G.

There is a spirit which I feel that delights to do
no evil, nor to revenge any wrong, but delights
to endure all things, in hope to enjoy its own
in the end. Its hope is to outlive all wrath and
contention, and to weary out all exaltation and
cruelty, or whatever is of a nature contrary to
itself. It sees to the end of all temptations. As
it bears no evil in itself, so it conceives none in
thoughts to any other. If it be betrayed, it bears
it, for its ground and spring is the mercies and
forgiveness of God. Its crown is meekness, its
life is everlasting love unfeigned; it takes its
kingdom with entreaty and not with contention,
and keeps it by lowliness of mind. In God alone
it can rejoice, though none else regard it, or
can own its life. It's conceived in sorrow, and
brought forth without any to pity it, nor doth
it murmur at grief and oppression. It never
rejoiceth but through sufferings; for with the
world's joy it is murdered. I found it alone,
being forsaken. I have fellowship therein with
them who lived in dens and desolate places
in the earth, who through death obtained this
resurrection and eternal holy life.

James Nayler, 1660
Quaker Faith & Practice 19.12

To Peter – another fruit of our partnership

The Author

Beth Allen grew up a Quaker in
north London, studied theology at
Nottingham University and married
an Anglican priest. She worked for the
Quakers at Friends House for 20 years
until 2005, mainly managing the work
of supporting Quaker meetings in the
Quaker Home Service department,
later Quaker Life, and then as General
Secretary of Quaker Communications.
Her Quaker work involved
considerable contact with other
churches and faiths, and handling
difficult issues such as child protection.
The many Quakers who have met
Beth will recognise the excitement she
has found in helping to maintain and
promote Quakerism.

Ground and Spring

Foundations of Quaker discipleship

Beth Allen

Swarthmore Lecture 2007

QUAKERbooks

First published May 2007

Quaker Books, Friends House, 173 Euston Road, London NW1 2BJ

www.quaker.org.uk

ISBN 978 0 901689 67 2

Cover design Hoop Associates
Book design and typesetting Golden Cockerel Press Ltd, London

Acknowledgements

Extract from "Bird of Heaven" by Sydney Carter reproduced by permission of Stainer & Bell Ltd.

"Agapé" by Oliver Postgate reproduced by kind permission of the author.

"The Rainbow" by Jill Slee Blackadder by kind permission of the author.

SCM Press for Dietrich Bonhoeffer, *Letters and Papers from Prison*.

Extract from "The Dream of the Rood" from *Early Christian Poetry: Translated into alliterative verse* by Charles William Kennedy, by permission of Oxford University Press.

Excerpt from "The Dry Salvages" in *Four Quartets*, copyright 1941 by T. S. Eliot and renewed 1969 by Esme Valerie Eliot, reprinted by permission of Harcourt, Inc., and Faber and Faber Ltd.

The "Bookmark" of Teresa of Avila is a version by Peter Daniels, based on Henry Wadsworth Longfellow's translation.

The Swarthmore Lecture

The Swarthmore Lectureship was established by the Woodbrooke Extension Committee at a meeting held 9 December 1907: the minute of the Committee providing for an "annual lecture on some subject relating to the message and work of the Society of Friends". The name Swarthmore was chosen in memory of the home of Margaret Fox, which was always open to the earnest seeker after Truth, and from which loving words of sympathy and substantial material help were sent to fellow workers.

The Lectureship continues to be under the care of Woodbrooke Quaker Study Centre trustees, and is a significant part of the education work undertaken at and from Woodbrooke.

The lectureship has a twofold purpose: first, to interpret to the members of the Society of Friends their message and mission; and second, to bring before the public the spirit, aims and fundamental principles of Friends. The lecturers alone are responsible for any opinions expressed.

The lectureship provides both for the publication of a book and for the delivery of a lecture, the latter usually at the time of Britain Yearly Meeting of the Society of Friends. A lecture related to the present book was delivered at Yearly Meeting in London on the evening of 5 May 2007.

The Swarthmore Lecture Committee can be contacted via the Clerk, c/o Woodbrooke Quaker Study Centre, 1046 Bristol Road, Selly Oak, Birmingham B29 6LJ.

Contents

Preface

"The scribe trained for the Kingdom of Heaven brings out of their treasure what is new and what is old" (Matthew 13:56) and if the treasure has been there a long time, we may be unsure where it came from. Behind many of my words lie the words of others – Julian of Norwich, Paul Tillich, George Herbert, Alan Richardson, Rowan Williams, and countless more who have fed into my thinking and reflection, to say nothing of 350 years of Quaker writing and talking, ministry and silence. Those readers who know the originals better than I will see words from others half-quoted and woven in.

I have worked with so many Friends who have shaped my thinking – thank you among many others to Jo Farrow, David Gray, Vera Dolton, Clifford Barnard, Anne Hosking, Jim Pym and Elsa Dicks. In particular, I have been grateful for earlier Swarthmore lecturers. Many of the concepts first voiced by Janet Scott, Christine Trevett, Eleanor Nesbitt, Helen Steven and others have become a part of my own thinking. Perhaps most of all, I am thankful for Chris Cook and Brenda Heales' lecture, *Images and Silence*.

I am grateful to all those who replied to the initial survey of discipline and practice. Margaret Allen, Frank Cranmer and Josie Stein all read and commented extensively on a first draft; they have saved me from several howlers but the responsibility for mistakes is mine, not theirs. Josef Keith of Friends House Library, London, patiently hunted up references.

The Swarthmore Lecture Committee prompted, corrected, encouraged and supported me, particularly through Brenda Heales and Michael Bliss; Deborah Padfield copy-edited and Peter Daniels, with other Quaker Communications staff, brought the book to publication. Working with Friends is such fun!

Finally, thanks as ever to Peter Allen for rock-solid support and piercing insights.

I have tried to use inclusive language, with the exception of direct quotations, and above all to be gender-neutral in referring to God. The New Revised Standard Version of the Bible is used unless specified otherwise. Some essential Quaker terms appear in the Glossary.

Introduction

Catch the bird of heaven
Lock him in a cage of gold;
Look again tomorrow,
And he will be gone.

Ah! the bird of heaven!
Follow where the bird has gone;
Ah! the bird of heaven!
Keep on travelling on.

Sydney Carter, 1969

Where can we find the bird of heaven – how can we keep the freedom of the Spirit? How do we travel on with the bird and with each other, confidently and faithfully? Are we free enough for the fresh, clear wind of the Spirit to lift us up?

Ours is a world of tension between religions, between religious and secular faiths and between understandings of what religious faith is. In such a world, Friends – like other seekers – search for some certainties, some foundations which are not cages for ourselves or for each other – or for the Spirit – and which might help us to live with integrity and passion. A study of that search is the basis of this book. For me, this is the search for God, not as an abstraction but as a living, loving, guiding presence in my life.

How can we think, worship and take action in integrity today? Can we find a definite ground for our beliefs, a resilient foundation for our way of life? How can we be faithful simultaneously to our inner selves, to the knowledge we have of psychology, physics and ecology, and also to our faith community's inherited teaching and its founding inspiration? How can we be faithful to the divine Spirit which we know from our past, and which calls us forward?

I hope – I believe – that some of the traditional Quaker styles of living, thinking and speaking might form a good pattern for our attempts to live truthfully and with integrity in faithful discipleship, and to work for peace, justice and the well-being of our planet.

This is an ambitious enterprise! But if we are to do big and strong things in a world which needs strong justice and deep compassion, we need tough, resilient theology and practice. We need a solid foundation to ground us as we reach for the ideals, the actions which will make peace and justice real today.

As Friends, we start and finish with meeting for worship. Several interlocking themes will be woven together in our consideration – creation, ruin and re-creation; truth and integrity; faithful challenge; discipleship and how we are faithful in it; leadership and authority; tension and calm; statements of belief; eternity holding time; silence and words holding each other; action and stillness.

Along the way, we will examine some of the words from the Quaker tradition; it is instructive to open them up, to find the metaphors hidden in them, examining the language structures we use with such familiarity that we often don't see their significance. Because they are couched in silence, Quaker words can carry huge meaning, and they hold much of our tradition and teaching.

I have found some mathematical and scientific models, images and ideas stimulating, but my treatment of them is not that of a specialist; my initial viewpoint is that of the student of theology. However, when we deal with the stuff of the universe, we have to look at the cross-fertilisation between disciplines and the relationship between science and faith. The arguments are all around us, not to be ignored. I hope others who know more will take this discussion further.

There are four questions which I find helpful in working with theological and philosophical thought:

- What experience lies behind this statement?
- What concept of God does this statement imply?
- What is God doing?
- How can I help?

Building with a varied collection of ideas and viewpoints is tricky. Our way of building a community, a meeting or a committee – or a book on Quaker thinking – is rather like building a dry-stone wall: we start with a collection of solid stones, but they are all of different shapes and sizes, some knobbly, some heavy, others thin. Some are foundation stones, others finish the structure off, one is just right for that awkward gap; the trick is to recognise how to use each stone in its right place.

I hope these varied ideas will be serviceable as an intelligible structure which may define a few fertile fields of thought, without fencing the Spirit in. Are we ourselves willing to be built with, to be used?

1. In the Beginning . . .

As we will be looking at the roots of our worship, our practice and our beliefs, a brief account of the ground of my own thinking will show some of the experience behind my words. I was born to Quaker parents, both from Birmingham; my father was brought up as an Anglican but came home to Quakerism around the time he met my mother. Both were conscientious objectors in the Second World War and members of the Friends Ambulance Unit. I was a child of peace, born just after V.E. Day. As a family we enjoyed international friendships with Russian, Chinese and American people; we welcomed ex-prisoners and children from broken homes and fractured families. We joined in peace and anti-nuclear demonstrations, and in one of my last memories of Dad, two days before he died, he was rewriting, in his hospital bed, the draft of a letter about the importance of the International Court of Justice. He grasped my hand and said urgently, "Beth, we must ban the bomb." We were members of Finchley Meeting, where my mother gave a great deal of time and love to the meeting's children.

So for them and for me, peace, disarmament, the meeting community and its children were always significant, but more important still was the silence in Meeting and the words which arose in it. What is happening here? I asked myself. What are we turning towards? How do we know when to speak in the silence? Whatever it was, it was so big that our family's life revolved round it. And this big thing had made my parents stand out for peace, against friends and family and the whole tenor of national thinking in the 1930s. So I searched *Christian Faith & Practice*, and wanted to go on asking the big questions; theology was the only thing I wanted to study at university.

As a young Quaker I had a huge advantage when starting theological study. I had a solid grounding in silent worship, and had studied religious education at school, but knew little hard doctrinal teaching. Thus I could read adult thought without too many childish interpretations to reject, and my faith was enlarged but not rocked.

Today, many people are searching for spirituality and religion without the solid base formerly given by school and Sunday school teaching, which can similarly be an advantage in that they come as adults without preconceptions.

I went to Nottingham University in the autumn of 1963, just after the publication of *Towards a Quaker View of Sex* and John Robinson's *Honest to God* – both of which were welcomed by many Friends as sound and usefully outspoken thinking. Friends were less worried than some by John Robinson's book because we didn't have credal bathwater to throw out from around the divine baby of experience.

I learnt in my first term to think in abstract terms, and to look critically at the Gospel narratives. I already knew how important it was to think and speak truthfully. Then I came home for Christmas and joined in rehearsals for Finchley Meeting's annual carol-singing round the streets of Woodside Park – stars and angels, kings and shepherds, "veiled in flesh the Godhead see" and all the rest. How could I sing these words with integrity? I chose to understand them as poetic truth, a crucially different path to the big ideas towards which I was fumbling. Perhaps the whole of my thinking since then is an elaboration of that early decision.

Because of our passionate search for truthfulness and integrity in our thought and speech, many Friends find language about God difficult, and since God is inseparable from Quaker thought, we know we have problems with shared language. Quakers who are non-theists are trying new ways of expressing inner experience, and their commitment to integrity of thought draws deeply on that traditional Quaker concern for truth; later chapters will explore the questions of imagery and experience more fully. I use the word "God" as a shorthand for all the poetic, philosophical and imaginative things that have been said and written about a divinity at once elusive but knowable, with us and beyond us, communicable but also beyond words. If the word "God" causes problems, is it possible to look beyond the difficulties to understand the positive experience?

My university department's staff paired the lone Quaker in a tutorial group with an Anglican monk who was training to be a priest. Peter and I never asked them why, but we've now been married for 39 years, an experience which is another foundation of my Quaker understanding. Peter's earlier journey included the Congregational Church and a personal commitment to Christianity which combined the influence of Billy Graham with that of an Anglo-Catholic girlfriend.

Peter started to come to Meeting to sit in silence with me, and I went to chapel to learn plainsong with him, finding that the music rose from the silence and deepened it, like ministry. We have each joined each other's denomination; Peter shares the life of the meeting, and I am an Anglican lay reader. Other people find this puzzling; for us, it's an expression in organisational terms of where and what we are, each linked to the other and to God.

I have learned about the Church in practice as a vicar's wife, through meeting people in need and in celebration, giving sandwiches to alcoholics on the vicarage doorstep in Holloway, fixing funerals, taking the banns for weddings, selling baby clothes at jumble sales for almost nothing to women with the grey pinched look of poverty, and having little money ourselves; sharing in the life of a loving and worshipping community; working with Black Pentecostal groups, Cypriot Orthodox and Tamil Christians; understanding the reality behind the caricature of the Church, and the people behind the slogans. Once when Peter was a curate, I was asked to speak about Quakers to the Mothers' Union; I produced the usual description of early Friends as I had learned it, and of the formalism and inadequacy of the Church of England in the seventeenth century. The wife of the vicar, my husband's boss, was a history graduate, and she was not pleased. "The Church wasn't totally unspiritual!" she said. "What about George Herbert?", and I realised how much we all deal in slogans and caricatures. Living in Truth means learning to build up as full as possible a picture of our own and other denominations, not just the truth of our own rebellion against them. God is bigger than the caricatures. If we all judge each other by our worst examples, how do Quakers fare?

I came to grasp in fact as well as theory the variety of a God who was bigger than the God of whom many Friends spoke. In the inner suburbs of London, people of all faiths and none are working for justice, for racial integration, for good housing, for decent services, for good education, for asylum seekers, in city farms, in playgroups, in advice centres. Many Quakers are in our inner cities as social workers, town planners, teachers, health professionals, and that is right for us, these are our jobs. The other denominations live there, they are "the church on the corner", God grounded in city life, a sign of hope and community. Once we were outside St David's, West Holloway, when a skinny girl of about eight went by; her brother had been baptised a week before; she had the sharp sassy look of the street-wise Islington child as she waved at the building, and "That's my church", she told her friend proudly. The Church of England, because of its commitment to the parish system, is earthed in the lives of ordinary people; in my life I have experienced it alongside people where they are, mixed in with the bustle and anonymity of inner London, the roughness of a council estate in Devon, the genteel edges of Salisbury, or the daily life of small towns in rural Wiltshire.

One crucial, bitter lesson was that God is distinct from any religious body of fallible human beings. As we moved from parish to parish and meeting to meeting, I learned not to put down roots in any house or building or organisational structure, only in people and in friendships – and in the Spirit.

Most of all, as a vicar's wife, I learned to trust God, in my own inner growth and in practical matters. However awful the situation, however huge and unmanageable the house, however overdrawn the bank balance and exhausting the daily trek to school, we had a solid shared foundation. Clothes came from jumble sales and from friends, food from Marks and Spencer's out-of-date donations; we could stretch out home-made pizza with cheap vegetables and live on cheap cuts – I went into our butcher's shop one day after Peter had been paid for a wedding, and said "I'm going to be wildly extravagant"; he grinned and replied, "You're going to buy *two* breasts of lamb!"

God was reliable. Or, to put it another way, by approaching life with an attitude of trust, we found a way of creating meaning out of whatever happened; trusting God shifted our attitude to life. The essence of it, for the two of us, was learning to live out in practice the theory we had learned together. This was true in our inward and outward lives. The practical and the theoretical amplified and illuminated each other; as John 7:17 puts it, "Jesus said, 'Anyone who resolves to do the will of God will know whether the teaching is from God.'" We were frustrated often, we were puzzled, but God led us, God provided, through people and institutions, family and friends. Then when we became more affluent, it became our turn to provide.

The children see it rather differently – a life of hand-me-downs and noble thinking gives you an appetite for bling, quality, good clothes and nice food, as well as habits of thrift and an understanding of all sorts of people.

It could be said that my thinking is just the product of my upbringing, my indoctrination through a lifetime of association with religious bodies, both the Church of England and the Society of Friends. I can only say that the habit of reflection which I learned in the quiet of meeting for worship has enabled me to make a clear and independent choice to go with some of what I learned as a child, and to think carefully and critically through other aspects of Quaker culture and nurture. Similarly, there are aspects of the institutional Church of England which I have chosen to take part in and agree with, and others that I choose to disagree with. My search has been for a mental and spiritual grounding on which I can build with integrity, and about which I can speak truthfully with commitment. I find this solid ground ultimately and only in God.

There is a story that once, when Francis of Assisi went by himself to spend time alone with God in quiet and solitude, his friend Brother Leo followed him, wanting to know how Francis used this time. He heard Francis repeating again and again, "God, who are you? And who am I?" (Moorman, 1963, p.106).

These two questions underlie much of the following discussion. Who are we, and on what do we build our own silence and thinking and action? Who is God, the ground of us all and of the universe? Francis sought to enter into the sufferings of Jesus, the anguish of the world, and if we are also searching for solid grounds for our thinking and our lives, we too must consider grief and pain. Francis came back from his time alone to live in community with his friends. As the bird of heaven flies through our lives and hearts, how do we live – individually and together – with energy, with springing new life, with change, fluidity and variety, in faithful discipleship?

2. Sharing the Work of Creation

Co-creators with God

We cannot think about God without struggling to understand "creation", the whole of the universe and ourselves as part of it. On the big scale, how the universe fits together, the stars, evolution, the climate systems of the earth, and human history; on the small scale, how my mind behaves inside my brain and my body; and in between those, how the meeting house plumbing works, how we all function as individuals and together. None of us can grasp all this alone; we rely on and learn from each other.

As human beings on Planet Earth, we are beginning to understand how we have ruined creation. Friends, like many others, are committed to changing the ways we behave so that we can live more gently and simply in accord with our world. Full discussion of that is another subject, but since contemplation and love of our creation is one of this book's underlying themes, our faithfulness in living out this growing testimony is a significant part of it. As we have developed Quaker thinking about living ecologically sound and integrated lives, we have gone back to the words of John Woolman, written in 1763:

> The Creator of the earth is the owner of it. He gave us being thereon, and our nature requires nourishment, which is the produce of it. As he is kind and merciful, we as his creatures, while we live answerable to the design of our creation, are so far entitled to a convenient subsistence that no man may justly deprive us of it . . . But he who with a view to self-exaltation, causeth some with their domestic animals to labour immoderately, and with the monies arising to him therefrom, employs others in the luxuries of life, acts contrary to the gracious design of the Creator, who is the true owner of the earth; nor can any possessions, either acquired or derived from ancestors, justify such conduct.
>
> *QF&P* 20.32

In this passage, John Woolman is arguing for economic justice, but his phrase "while we live answerable to the design of our creation" has a fuller meaning; I interpret it to mean that we can live with integrity to our own distinctive nature, answering, responding to and fitting in with the truth about ourselves, individually and corporately, as well as the truth about the world we are in.

We cannot forget our painful knowledge of how people don't behave, how communities, families and meetings function badly and harmfully – but we also know how we humans can, often at great cost, reconcile ourselves with each other and with our interior selves, re-creating each other and our own hearts. Creation includes brokenness, often to the point of utter destruction, and healing too – healing which sometimes has to be acceptance of total loss. We shall explore this more deeply later.

We are partners in creation with each other and with God; we share in it as co-creators. J.R.R. Tolkien wrote of our part in the process of creation: "We make still by the law in which we're made . . . We make in our measure and in our derivative mode, because we are made: and not only made, but made in the image and likeness of a Maker" (Tolkien, 1964, pp.54 and 56).

We are co-creators with God when we create a meal, a home, an effective team of staff, a sound maths lesson, a child's knitted dress, a turbine blade. We are perhaps even more co-creators with the divine Spirit when we re-create – whether we dig over a neglected allotment and make it productive, or counsel a traumatised asylum seeker, or bring sense and order into a chaotic pile of receipts and cheque book stubs, or enable diplomats to put together a treaty on land mines. To make and re-make these powerful, beautiful things, we use a great deal of inward training, often using skills and disciplines we have learnt and internalised so much that we find it natural to be faithful to them.

We often think of creativity as the solitary expression of our inmost soul, but many of the creations which have made our Quaker community grow in the last few years have been shared enterprises which no one person could produce, and we have grown as we have made them together – the Quaker Tapestry, the Leaveners' productions, *Quaker Faith & Practice* itself, our Yearly Meetings and Summer Gatherings. In order to create together, we gladly hand over our precious autonomy to the authority of the group, the authority of the event, the Clerk, conductor, or skilled peacemaker, and we are prepared to be part of the group. We are learning together to use the disciplines and language of music and painting and theatre; this re-creates our communities and simultaneously brings us more deeply into the ground of all this creativity, the silence and words of God.

I see this participation in the creative process as the practical expression of our theological commitment to and exploration of life lived with the Spirit. Francis Howgill says of the early experience of the Quaker community, "The Kingdom of God did gather us and catch us all, as in a net" (QF&P 19.08). The Spirit is the sparkling network of new creative energy between us all, the threads of love, of friendship, of shared passion and commitment, the web of shared work, learning and understanding, words and silences we are gathered and caught in together. If the Spirit is the artist who is creating us as a community, we can enter into that artist's vision and work with it, and we apply the tools of discernment and truthful communication which help us to work together with each other and with the Creator. This is "the fellowship of the Holy Spirit", and this we know.

Tolkien, thinking hierarchically, puts our creativity under God's creativity and calls us "sub-creators". Paul of Tarsus speaks of us – translating literally from his Greek – as "fellow-workers together with God" (2 Corinthians 6:1) as we create communities together, and this to my mind is preferable; though I do find *The Lord of the Rings* easier to read than the Letter to the Ephesians.

In the poetic narrative of Genesis we, *homo fabricans*, share in the work of creation, playing in the mud and mess on the ground with God, making man and woman – Adamah/Adam, the Hebrew word for "ground" and Havvah/Eve, Hebrew for "life" – out of the earth together, with all that flows from them and us, gardening in and caring for the world.

This fits with the image of God as "the Ground of our Being"; "ground" is another metaphor based in creation, including the mud and the earth. I interpret this phrase to point towards God as the basic energy which makes up and flows through every particle of the universe, the lively stuff of which it is all formed, the tension and buzz which holds it all together but which also is a solid foundation for stillness and rest. We can stretch our minds to follow today's scientists as they work in the creative mud with string theory and particle physics; what physicists and laypeople share is the knowledge that the universe behaves itself: whatever the energies between particles, a glass of water set down on a table still stays in the glass, on top of the table. The order of creation is predictable – two bricks added to two bricks make four bricks – and where it seems wild and uncertain, amongst the unknowns of general relativity and quantum theory, we are studying it, developing models more in accordance with what seems mathematically to work: a deeper reliability.

The poet-writers of the Genesis narratives were convinced that creation is fundamentally good; it springs from, includes and embraces chaos, play and wildness, but is also rooted in order; John's Gospel and the Book of Proverbs add the insight that underlying creation we can find wisdom, reason and intelligence, the *logos* ("word, reason"). The creative Light and Word are essentially good; it is good for us to see, to understand and name creation, to rejoice in it and look after it. These key elements from Genesis are the bedrock of Judaeo-Christian understandings of the world and are shared with the other Abrahamic religion, Islam.

As we answer Francis of Assisi's question, "Who am I?", we are meditating on some of the mysteries of creation: our own individuality, our place in a community and in a complex, varied world. And we are not just looking at this as a static picture. The flowers on the table in the centre of our meeting for worship are growing, living and dying; the "days" in the Genesis myth underline the insight that creation takes place in time, bringing temporality, change and movement into eternity. The seeds germinate and grow, the flower matures and new seeds are fertilised, the plant fades, dies, is dissolved into its elements, and makes the seed-bed for new flowers.

The Genesis creation story also includes the insight that it is not good for a human being to be alone (Genesis 2:18). Partnership, friendship and community are there from the start and it is our experience, as a Society, that gay and straight partnerships are equally truthful and integrated parts of creation. We are created in such a way that the Divine can speak to us through the physical. Newcomers at Quaker Quest often remind us that for many people sexual experience is a re-creative experience of the Divine. This is nothing new; the Song of Songs celebrates our sexuality within the biblical canon, and *The Da Vinci Code* was popular partly because it explicitly welcomed this

possibility. People have forgotten that the experience and the concept
are both considerably older than the book.

A hidden God

Somehow God is content to remain as the background to much of
creation. As a young theology student I felt I would understand more
of God's nature when I too had a baby and shared in the creation of
new life. Before Katy was born I imagined that her birth would be
a great religious experience. It wasn't; it was a very human experience,
joyful, hard work, quite messy and thrilling; and afterwards I asked
Peter, "Where was God in all that?" and he replied, "God is there, but
He doesn't push Himself forward," quoting Isaiah 45:15: "Truly, you are
a God who hides himself."

So the answer to "What is God doing?" has to be preceded by
"What are we actually looking for?" If God is hidden in creation, we
can understand the way creativity works from several angles at once.
A picture – perhaps Rembrandt's *The Adoration of the Shepherds*
– is an arrangement of pigments and oils, chemicals and vegetable
matter on a canvas, and simultaneously a powerful emotional
statement of numinous wonder, created by an experienced hand
and a visionary mind. The birth of a child, or the birth of a star, is
a physical event which can be described in biological terms or in the
language of astrophysics, and it is simultaneously a manifestation,
an epiphany, a showing of the wonder and immensity of the power
of God. Healing of body and soul can come as a result of prayer
and simultaneously through skill, care, medicine and counselling.
A rainbow is totally explicable in scientific terms – and at the same
time, its message of the mixture of sun and rain, sadness and joy, can
give us hope.

We can look at the flowers on our meeting house table and say,
"This also is Thou; but neither is this Thou" – a phrase which seems to
track back through C.S. Lewis to St Ephrem the Syrian in the fourth
century. Because we look through them, we transcend the flowers and
know that God is in them and beyond them too, in their atoms and
essence, in their springing life, in the gardener who grew them and the
person who arranged them.

The idyllic picture of life in Paradise, harmony and beauty all
around, creation before the Fall, was a big part of the experience and

thinking of early Quakers. George Fox tells us that "Now I was come up through the flaming sword, into the Paradise of God. And all the creation gave another smell to me than before" (Fox, 1985, p.27). The equality of the sexes which early Friends lived out was intended to express a restoration of the paradisal state, man and woman together, helpsmeet before the Fall. The plain language they used equally to all was also a restoration of the paradisal language. So the image of creation restored has been part of Quaker vision and thinking from our beginnings. A hopeful and confident understanding of the "design of our creation" is still a big element in Quaker thinking today, linking in with our positive affirmation of our belief in "that of God in everyone" (QF&P 19.32). When Friends originally used this phrase, they meant that we are created in such a way that we can respond to God, with the implication that God, human beings and the created world are capable of having a relationship, a conversation; they are not alien to each other. "That of God in everyone" in technical terms is our self-understanding as human beings, the British Quaker doctrine of humanity, our answer to "Who am I?"

Where do the images come from? As we ask the big questions about life and death, we often make word-pictures, elementary theology, about our own situation and God's activity in it. We use the mental materials we have to hand, our own experiences and what matters most to us. In one episode of the television series *Steptoe and Son*, Albert and Harold talked about Albert's death as "going to the great scrap-yard in the sky". For the Vikings, heaven was Valhalla, a great hall where they drank mead and swapped stories of past battles together. The tramps' song, "The Big Rock Candy Mountain", pictures Paradise as soda-water fountains, cigarette trees and warm weather; for Sydney Smith, it was eating pâté de foie gras to the sound of trumpets, not my idea of bliss at all. Images of Paradise are not necessary, but they illustrate the fact that we use images, often unknowingly – and I recall a spectacular failure when I tried to teach a group of young children to see heaven in abstract terms as anywhere where people are loving and kind, and received a stack of homework about drinking from fountains of lemonade and riding ponies all day long.

As we play with our ideas of God, what images and metaphors do we use, sometimes unthinkingly? What experience lies behind our word-pictures? How do we assess the validity of our images?

Because schooldays are such a formative and communal experience for most of us, our metaphors may be drawn from that time. For example, my old mental picture of the mythical disclosure of Ultimate Justice, the "Last Judgement", was based on memories of school prize-givings in my distant past. Plainly it wouldn't be exactly like them – but the essential element for me was the public acknowledgement, by an authority of some sort, of the qualities and achievements of individual people. There are elements in this picture which need to be tested and discarded – perhaps I need to discard the picture totally – but that is easier to do when I realise where the imagery is coming from. And I can throw out the picture without throwing out the eternal truth I am reaching for. I realised I had an inadequate picture of ultimate justice when, years ago, I felt an injustice had been done; I found I was saying, out loud but fortunately when I was alone, "And it's all written down in a big book, and one day everyone will read what you have done!" I now use much less specific language about ultimately bringing everything into the Light.

The test is, what concept of God underlies the image we are using? Is it good enough, is it big enough? And if we can recognise that a concept is not good enough, can we see that it is pointing towards something bigger than itself, something which might be more adequate? "God as headmistress" is not enough – can we add a few other images, drawn from positive experiences of authority? God as Clerk of the meeting, God as manager, God as driving instructor, God with the compelling call of a crying baby, God with the galvanising authority of the sight of bombed cities? Do these metaphors point towards a picture of the leadings of the Eternal breaking through into our lives? What do each of us reach for as our ultimate image, and why?

This is a translation of the Quaker understanding of the sacraments into the world of ideas and images. We understand creation to be such that the Divine can be significantly present to us in any shared meal. Similarly, in the world of thought, all imagery can point beyond itself to a deeper reality, to God. We can play with the models and images, we can build with them as long as we know they are just models – and then we test the results of our play against the realities of life.

"God, who are you?" One foundation of our thinking could be a God who is bigger than our thought can compass, who underlies creation, who gives the Divine for us to grasp and who invites us to be co-creators ourselves, as we share in the work of making and remaking the world.

3. The Grounds for our Silence

Why silence?

Francis' double question is a useful one: "God who are you, and who am I?" We need to keep asking it. It takes us straight into our experience and understanding of the roots of Quaker worship – to those moments when we are attending particularly to God and to our relationship with God, in our distinctive silence.

What is the ground of Quaker silence and of our thinking about it? When we sit down together in meeting for worship, we wait. We often say we are waiting on God. For me, the essence of Meeting, from the human angle, is our commitment to sit together and support each other in our shared attentive looking towards God in action. And it is here, in the laboratory of our worship, that we put many of our fundamental Quaker concepts most clearly into practice. Meeting for worship is the paradigm for much of our Quaker experience, the setting where we see the essentials in a small compass, and where we learn. Since we are seeking to understand the action of the divine Spirit, let us look at meeting for worship from this angle.

We create our meetings as human beings, working together with the Spirit. This for me is the absolute fundamental, the ground of the ground. The God to whom we turn in quiet is waiting for us, as we wait for God; and we can reach out in our hearts and simply meet God in stillness. This simple, one-sentence discovery is the energy and dynamic, the pause and hush within our whole organisation and structure. This is why, in Quaker Quest, we can explain Quaker worship in a few words to newcomers who have never tried it before, and then go into a deep silence together; this is why our children can hold Meeting; this is why in January 1985 we could worship in a crowded courtroom as the Clerks of Meeting for Sufferings were tried for withholding tax; this is why, in August 1938, Rufus Jones, George Walton and Robert Yarnall could sink into gathered worship in a waiting room in the headquarters of the Gestapo (Vining, 1958, p.291). This is why we don't need to talk about it a great deal. We just need to do it.

One paradox about this dynamic pause is that we choose to talk about it so much; in our discussions, Friends have discovered some principles which help us in our worship.

If we understand that the Spirit of God is content to work through us according to the pattern of our creation, to use our outer world as the medium for the Divine, then ordinary physical human things like sitting comfortably, or having enough fresh air, are some of the basics. We all know that in theory we can worship anywhere and transcend any circumstances; in practice, we learn to do this by becoming accustomed to and practised in ordinary Quaker worship. A solid diet of the ordinary is a great help if we have to cope with the unusual – and sometimes a good corrective to it.

Once we are comfortable and settled, which may take some time, we make ourselves available to the Spirit. The French word *disponible* expresses the attitude we take at this point, and I often find myself repeating it silently in meeting for worship. The word conveys an attitude of attentive availability – ready like a tool in the toolbox, like a spare part on a shelf. In a meeting for business or a meeting for learning I see this more vividly; I picture myself and what I bring to the meeting as a deck of cards in the hand of God, fanned out so that I am aware of what is available within me, and there to be played or not, as needed and as the discussion develops. This is an odd image for me as I haven't played card games since childhood.

Being real

We all have such a great deal of experience to bring to Meeting and to Quaker business – knowledge from the world of our own specialism, our own work, our understanding of the experience of seeking for the Divine, our awareness of children, our sense of how the group behaves. All sorts of skills come in here. I once worked with the Clerk of a big committee, an enthusiastic bridge-player, and I commented that her amazing awareness of the group round the table might be linked with her card-playing expertise; she replied, "Well, my bridge has actually improved since I took up this clerkship!"

However, if I have come to worship in great need or I'm a newish Quaker, or if I have a major issue to think over, then I am not *disponible*; I am relying on others to hold the stillness round me. But it is important to bring the need. We are free to be wholly our real selves in worship. Do you ever catch yourself thinking, "Oh, I can't have that thought, I'm in Meeting", and pushing it down so that you are acceptable and nice and quakerly as you sit there? I remember the first meeting for worship we held in our house in Holloway. I prepared the room carefully, picking up the odd child's shoe and cat's blanket. The children had been playing with their toys and near the fireplace I found a model soldier, a small plastic crusader in armour; "Oh dear, we can't have anything military in a room where we are to have a Quaker gathering," I thought. Afterwards I realised that I was trying to sanitise the whole room, trying (hopelessly) to pretend that we were a perfect quakerly family who would give no offence to anyone. If we are to worship with integrity, with our whole selves, we cannot be sanitised. We are human, and to be human is to be messy, to be earthed, to eat and drink and fail and succeed, to grieve and rage and exult as well as to be quiet and content. We bring all of this to Meeting.

The parallel failing is to play ourselves down, to deny and hide our strength and capacity. Often we force this on each other in a false egalitarianism. I once asked a very senior social worker, a newish attender, if she ever spoke of her expertise with other local Friends. "Oh no, they would feel I was boasting." It has been common for members of our national committees to keep quiet at local level about their national involvement; they are sensitive to a spoken or unspoken reaction of "who does she think she is, to be on a national committee?"

This is a corporate failure of confidence. I was interested to notice the eagerness with which the British Quaker community received the words of Marianne Williamson quoted by Nelson Mandela at his inauguration in 1994: "Your playing small doesn't serve the world. There's nothing enlightened about shrinking so that other people won't feel insecure around you" (Williamson, 1992). We felt as a community that this spoke to us, and I sense that since hearing that message we have become more assertive. Perhaps we are beginning to learn its lesson, and to bring our strengths to our Quakerism.

A Friend of long experience, Jo Farrow, said to me once, "The Psalms are about being real before God." They have been used in conversation with God for some three thousand years. "O Lord, why do you cast me off? Why do you hide your face from me? Wretched and close to death from my youth up, I suffer your terrors; I am desperate" (Psalm 88:14–15). "Blessed are those who, going through the vale of misery, use it for a well, and the pools are filled with water" (Psalm 84:6, *Book of Common Prayer*). This is not sanitised, tidied-up religion – the writers of the Psalms are energetic in their passionate relationship with God. Can we bring these honest, angry and miserable words and feelings into our own discussions with the Spirit?

The ground of our worship is a God who meets us as we are. We rightly reject, in our Quaker understanding, any other human being as a go-between in our relationship with God. But we often create a tidied-up version of ourselves to meet God and each other in Meeting, a mask which we can mentally hold in front of our faces in case God, or other Friends, or worse still we ourselves, might actually see the uneasy, floundering, tired person we really are. If we are not really there, God cannot really meet us. God calls us into being real, to be truthful. We minister this truthfulness, this call to integrity, to each other.

I recall two of my most breathtaking experiences of Quaker truth-telling. I was accustomed, as the manager of a central Quaker department and as an Elder in my meeting, to going beyond other people's words to me and understanding them at a deeper level. Then, once in a local Elders' meeting, and once in a meeting with my colleagues in Friends House, other Friends did this to me. I said something, I can't now remember what; all I can recall is that I was understood and challenged at a deeper level, and reduced to silence by the Quaker ability to see beyond the mask. And if we Friends can do this lovingly, still more so can the Spirit.

So another foundation of our worship is our own integrity within it, our own willingness to be wholly present in all the fullness of our strength and all our inadequacy. As communities, can we also learn to accept each other's strengths and expertise? As individual Friends, can we make all the cards in our hand available to the Spirit and to each other?

Elements of old Quaker language preserve the insight of earlier generations into our understanding of God's work. In Meeting, God's action is important, not our own. We "wait upon God". Today, probably more than in the past, we are reluctant to speak directly about God, for some of us feel great hesitation about naming the Divine. Listen carefully to Friends talking about their experience of ministry and of other action; we often use indirect speech or verbs in the passive voice. We say, "I was led to . . . " or "We are convinced that . . . ", without specifying who or what led or convinced us. This can be simultaneously a scrupulously truthful refusal to say that God led us, when we can be only partially but not totally certain, and a reverent avoidance of over-familiarity with the Divine. It's also an attractive reaction against too much certainty. Friends of an earlier period took this even further; describing a Meeting, they might say that "Isaac Braithwaite appeared in ministry" because it was not possible to say with truth whether Isaac was actually ministering or not: only God knew. Similarly, a Friend would not say afterwards, "Thank you for your ministry", but "I was thankful for your ministry" – thankful to the divine Spirit, not to the human speaker. Notice again the indirect turn of phrase.

Jesus used the same sort of reverent side-stepping; he often spoke of "the Kingdom" or "heaven" when a cruder approach would say "God", and he used the passive voice: "you are forgiven . . . ", "you are healed . . . " The traditional Quaker language preserves the insights of earlier generations, but needs to be broken open today so that its original meaning can be rediscovered.

There are two results of this Quaker form of speech – we can forget who is leading us, and others can assume that we have no place for the Divine in our thinking. But in addition, when we occasionally use very direct speech – "the Spirit of Christ, which leads us into all truth, will never move us to fight . . . " (QF&P 24.04) – it comes over with extra power.

Within the stillness

This is not a campaign for old language, but for the insight contained in the language – that the God about whom we so cheerfully and easily talk is not "God in our pocket". This is another fundamental in our worship and thinking. As Mr Beaver says of Aslan, "He's wild, you know. Not like a *tame* lion" (Lewis, 1987, p.166). The God before whom we sit in silence is transcendent, beyond space and time, holding all the universe in being in all its complexity – God to whom we respond with awe and wonder and respect. We need big enough words to describe God, our minds need to be enlarged, elastic and strong enough at least to try to frame the Divine and convey our experience.

This is the God before whom Chartres Cathedral was built, and the stone circle at Callanish, the God for whom Mozart wrote his C Minor Mass, and Brahms his Requiem. We all know of elements in our culture and in many other cultures which reduce us to a tiny squeak of a voice, or to silence, as we participate in them or stand before them in wonder. Part of the Quaker genius is to welcome God in the domestic, the everyday – the architectural model for older meeting houses is often the vernacular, the style of local houses – and one result is that we are unfamiliar with the experience of meeting God in big groups of people or in the soaring heights of huge structures. Does this lead us to domesticate the Divine, to forget the transcendent, to deal only in small visions and little details?

The inner spaces within each of us are mental and spiritual worlds huge beyond our imagining. As we sit in our small worshipping circle, we bring these worlds together in one great interlocking pattern: we hold in our hearts all the people we treasure, and what they might come to be in the future; libraries of books, poems and all the words we could write and read; galleries of pictures and all the music we could listen to and create ourselves; all the experience we have packed into our lives and the thoughts we have explored; all the discoveries we ourselves have made.

We can feel the infinite multiplicity of creation in all its potential, we can imagine and so, perhaps, help to create new possibilities and new worlds. In the silence we are held in privacy and yet in company. We can think the unthinkable, explore depths of anguish, misery and joy, try out radical thought and sense a call to new endeavour. As we meet together, our inner worlds can combine so that new links are made, new cross-fertilisations take place and new life springs up. It is a wonderful time to open our inner eyes, to see visions and to dream dreams together – and all this potential is part of us, and so also part of the Divine.

In her recent book *Keeping God's Silence*, our Friend Rachel Muers, who teaches theology at Exeter University, suggests that the silence of God into which we can go in Meeting and elsewhere is the silence of God the listener, hearing us as a trusted friend listens to us, with full and loving attention (Muers, 2004, p.60).

So the foundations of our worship are the nature of God and our own nature; our conviction of the primacy of God's action; our belief that God is listening to us when we listen to God; and our experience that deep silence can take us to the eternal, focusing and strengthening us to act with the Spirit. Meeting for worship expresses most clearly the Quaker conviction that we wait for and rely on God, and God alone. As we release the inner wellsprings of Love in the Spirit, we let the living water flow within us, and our Meetings can become life-giving fountains of silence.

This is why Meeting is central to Quaker life. So what words of stillness can hold and reflect and pass on our experience? What quiet words, what peaceable actions are channels for the rivers of living water? How do we develop so that we can daily live in peace and quietness within our hearts and in the world? And then, how do we leap with the Spirit, fly with the bird of heaven and re-create a new world in justice and integrity?

4. God at Work?

What's the evidence for the action of God? One of the central tenets of Quakerism – and one of the bases of this book – is that we wait for the movement of God's Spirit, that God acts, that God works; so where do we see this happening? If our ever-creative God is indeed working through the ordinary pattern of the universe and in the processes of everyday life, can we identify in our experience any action which we might consider that God initiates – which could be picked out and labelled "God at work"?

This dangerous question has been answered so tragically, both in the past and in our own times, that we must approach it with extreme caution. Yet we can at least attempt a sketch of possible thoughts about it, and the beginning of a reasoned approach, arising from our shared experience as British Friends. In this chapter we look at God as God is perceived by us, seekers and people of faith, not as God is in Godself (an alternative to "himself" I found first in Rachel Muers' writing).

A common Quaker experience is that of an inner nudge, or leading. We feel this as a thought or a prompting which will not go away: "Ring up Susan", or "Why not offer yourself as an ecumenical accompanier in Israel and Palestine?" Our first Advice reminds us to "Take heed, dear Friends, to the promptings of Love and Truth in your hearts. Trust them as the leadings of God" (*Advices & Queries* 1). In other words, we will be led to do good and loving things; an inner prompting to make a snappy retort or to send a quick hurtful email, however immediately satisfying, is unlikely to be a leading from God. The inner nudges are also the promptings of Truth, and therefore will accord with the integrity of our individual life; an accountant is unlikely to be truly led to break professional confidentiality, and a right leading will use and extend our existing skills and capabilities.

What follows is simply my personal interpretation of what I have seen.

Sitting in Yearly Meeting around 40 years ago, I heard Stanley Keeble tell us that since our taxes were used to finance military preparations for war, as a matter of conscience we should refuse to pay a portion of that tax, and I heard us dismiss this as an idealistic and pointless gesture. But Stanley kept on saying it. As a member of Meeting for Sufferings in the early 1980s, I supported the concern of those members of Friends House staff who asked us to test the law on this and, as their employer, to withhold 12 per cent of their tax. Later, as a staff member, I too asked for this. Together, staff and employer, we followed this complex concern through the twists and turns right up to the European Commission on Human Rights.

This concern met all our tests. The two crucial ones, it seems to me, are first that it nagged at us, it kept coming back, and secondly that when we pulled the string, it kept on coming. There was a next step we could take. So we went on keeping the idea alive, and eventually the idea grew its own separate organisation, Conscience – the Peace Tax Campaign – and the initiative passed to others.

This is how I see the Spirit acting, working with and through each and all of us. The whole process – the individual passion, the initial ridicule, and then the sense that something will be worked on – makes its way through our system, with each part of the Quaker machine playing its part; it continues either until we have finished this job and can say as George Fox said, "Now I am clear, I am fully clear" (*QF&P* 41.29), or until a concern that is bigger than us goes beyond us and the thinking is spread, and has its own effect. In Jesus' imagery, the Kingdom of Heaven is like yeast in dough – it is hidden, and takes time to develop. Similarly, our decision to follow the leading of the Spirit in a concern is a declaration of God's primacy and authority, and a commitment to live by the truths of the Kingdom of Heaven; this too is initially hidden, but its effects are seen and used.

If we neglect the leading, or delay in our response to it, we miss the crucial time, in the old Quaker word the "opportunity"; and either the initiative passes to others who do respond, or the action needed is not taken – so we miss a chance to build the Kingdom.

We have often seen this pattern. Various concerns have started off as tender seedlings in the Quaker greenhouse, and are then transplanted to grow big outside when they are strong enough – Alternatives to Violence, and Circles of Support and Accountability, among many others. The Ecumenical Accompaniment Programme in Palestine and Israel shows the hallmarks – a small project, faithfully followed, where our first initiative moved to a different level as we co-operated with the other churches through the World Council of Churches, with Quaker insights, style and management.

I have talked about the big things because I have seen some of them develop through our recent history. The Spirit also operates in the local life of a Quaker meeting and in our individual lives. It was an early Quaker maxim to "despise not the day of small things" (Zechariah 4:10). We learn to work with the Spirit in small things first, then we are sometimes asked to work on bigger things. We all have our own experience of faithfulness in local initiatives and the daily experience of God's hidden action, in mundane details as well as in the whole tenor of our lives.

Learning discernment

As ever in Quaker matters, discernment is the key, and we know how to do that. The fact that we often don't bother to discern carefully doesn't invalidate our knowledge. We are not short of knowledge or of guidance; what we are short of is the will to live by it: the guts to leave other things and concentrate on the "one thing needful". "Purity of heart," said Søren Kierkegaard, "is to will one thing" (Kierkegaard, 1961).

Meeting for worship is the training ground, where we learn how to discern the right way forward and to work with the Spirit. We learn to recognise what is of God by watching others speak and act, and by acting and speaking ourselves – and by keeping silent.

Here my own experience has developed. The first time I was led to minister I felt I was being battered with pillows; I did not follow the leading, and came away from Meeting utterly drained by the effort of resisting. Over the years the leading became more understandable: the words were there and would not go away, and my heart beat faster; I learned only to minister when I truly felt led. There is no one single way of testing this leading. Because we operate in varied ways we feel the nudge in different ways and have to learn our own signals. For example, I have never "found myself on my feet" in the way that some Friends have described. For me there is always a conscious choice. I think that our experience of following leadings develops; more recently I have only felt the beating heart after I've spoken, which is rather disconcerting; I now have to test the leading less physically and more inwardly.

Friends rarely speak of this but a study would be interesting, and we could include similar non-Quaker experiences too. Margaret Cunliffe, an Anglican deaconess, describes the experience of leading in ministry in terms we recognise; she was in the middle of preaching a sermon when she saw someone come in at the back of the church; she felt moved to put in a few unplanned sentences, and later found that they spoke exactly to the newcomer's condition. A study of discernment might usefully include the methods of discernment and assessment that Friends use in "non-religious" settings. How do these relate to our experience in a Quaker context? Is this another case where the religious and the secular are the same experience described in different languages? And how do other people speak of their experience of concern and leadings? What is prompting them?

Following a prompting to speak in worship is quite public, and if a meeting discusses its worship, it is helpful to everyone to hear the piercing observations of those whose ministry Sunday by Sunday is usually silent. Sometimes a private word is appropriate. I always valued the words of a committee member to me: "When you speak, I don't feel you are always led by the Spirit." And years ago a wise older Friend, Margaret L. McNeill, listened to me ranting on about something. When I ran out of words, she said gently, "Beth, remember that you are *one* of God's gifts to the Society of Friends." As we watch the Spirit working in ourselves and in each other, and in our communities of meetings and committees, we can help each other to refine our own discernment.

Sometimes, instead of feeling the push inwardly, in our own hearts, the leading comes through another person suggesting something to us or asking us to do something, but we need to confirm this outward leading by looking for an inward answering. Often, Friends ask us to take on a routine job which just keeps our little bit of the Quaker world functioning, part of "the day of small things" (*QF&P* 19.43; Zechariah 4:10). This too can be a leading. In 1990 an American Quaker pastor, Margaret Benefiel, told a British Quaker conference on ministry: "Remember, if it is burdensome and oppressive it is probably not from God. The God who calls us also gives us the resources to do the task we are called to. The hallmarks of the Friend responding to his or her call should be courage, energy and joy" (*Equipping for Ministry* p.23). Finding courage to do the routine stuff cheerfully is also part of following a leading!

I've never forgotten a clear experience of one Friend leading worship. The Quaker Society at Nottingham University had a regular weekly meeting for worship on Tuesday lunchtimes, and one day about seven of us were sitting in a rather unsettled quiet, when one of our group came in. He sat down and within half a minute we were all inwardly stilled. We were led by him as he followed the Spirit among us to where we all wanted to go, though we couldn't find the way before.

My experience of God is chiefly of leadings, usually a leading to speak, sometimes a leading to action and to take up some work. Occasionally I sense a leading to lay down a task, or to take up or lay down a way of life. These things are seen most clearly when they change.

For example, when our children were small and we were living on a small wage in Islington, it seemed right to learn to rely on God, working through other people, for our material needs; I formulated each need in my mind and trusted the Spirit and the angels, and what we needed was offered, food, clothes, a pram, a holiday. Then later, the children were at school, I got a part-time job with a salary, and quite clearly I knew we had to change from this pattern – there was a sense that "you're on your own now, because you can be", and the flow dried up. Of course this can all be understood as projection, but the pram was real! And it lasted a good many years until we too gave it away.

Less tangible was the vocation as a lay reader in the Church of England. This came over the washing up one day – maybe things come during the washing up because it is a soothing mechanical process, or maybe it's just that some people spend a lot of time washing up . . . Anyway, it came as a new possibility which used my skills; the vocation was tested in the usual way and it was fulfilling. The hardest part for me was putting on the clothes – it seemed the most unquakerly bit of all I was doing – but one Quaker thing about my vocation as a reader is that it is a job for a lay person, not a priest, and I like that. At the same time, I was appointed as an Elder by my local meeting. I particularly recall two Sundays; on one, I was one of the two Elders who had to sit at the front and close meeting for worship, and I realised that during that hour my job was just holding the frame for everyone else's worship. On the next Sunday I was taking the first half of the service at St David's Church, West Holloway, and realised that it was just the same job – holding the frame for everyone else. In the jargon, an enabling, facilitative leadership, helping people, as we were helped at Nottingham, to go where they want to go.

But when my job became a lot busier, it was just not possible to serve as a lay reader in this way, and after about 18 years a vocation which I had thought would last for a lifetime just dried up. An odd experience, but in Quaker terms I had "outrun my guidance" and the calling changed. Another 12 years later, when the church we are now linked with was losing its vicar and appealed for "anyone who has skills which can help us to be prepared to help", I felt my dormant calling stir again.

Being available

"Fellow-workers together with God" (2 Corinthians 6:1) is a phrase I return to repeatedly as a description of what all this feels like. And the God I see behind all this is a God who is active, who works with and through us, inviting but not demanding our help. Perhaps some relevant images of the Divine for us today could be the divine Spirit as the encouraging facilitator, the guiding manager, the enabling Clerk? The essential element in these roles is respect for our capacity, for our gifts. God cannot be less than the best we know.

These leadings can come to us as meetings and committees, not just to us as individuals. We know in our hearts a great deal about the corporate worshipping and praying life of a meeting and a committee, though we don't often talk of it. The committee of the Friends Prayer League recorded its experience in 1914:

> The committee, like the individual, needs time to think and it needs an attitude of mind and soul which can make it able to receive increasingly what is of God about its work . . . Individually the faith of most of us is too weak sufficiently to grasp the promise "Behold, I do a new thing" (Isaiah 43:19) but a committee which grasps with corporate faith such a promise is the committee which will have a spirit of adventure in attempting the humanly impossible. And those who thus trust God discover God.
>
> *CF&P* 357

God also works through less conscious leadings. "What I see as God at work, other people say is coincidence. All I can say is, when I pray, coincidences happen." Whoever first said these words expressed the experience of many. Could it be that in prayer we put ourselves into the flow of God's energy rather than ignoring it, fighting it or refusing it; so we make possible the leadings and the coincidences? Practising prayer, in the variety of ways we do it, helps us to be available, *disponible*, as we are in worship; we may be used or we may not.

We can re-interpret the old concept of the "righteousness" of God as a dynamic rather than a static idea. Often if we think of someone as "righteous" we picture them as standing firm and unmoveable with an off-putting moral certainty. If our loving God is dynamic, righteousness begins to look more like a strong energy which acts for justice, puts things right, puts them in the flow of life, keeps them in a living cycle of being. I picture a flag streaming in the wind – the wind of the Spirit – which if we are open to it can stream through our lives and our meetings, and our world. Or could it be that God gently and subtly shifts and changes the flow of energy within us and within the world, as acupuncturists and other healers apply their skills to shift the energies already within us? This is a different sort of dynamic, a more co-operative mode of intervention.

We sometimes speak as if our experience of leadings is beyond our ordinary living of life. There is a story ascribed to John Wesley, of a day when on one of his frequent journeys he fell in with a Quaker and suggested that they should travel together. The Friend agreed, but said as they set out, "I should warn you that I only speak under the direct inspiration of the Holy Spirit." Wesley noted that evening, "We had a very dull day." Everyday life is part of the life of the Spirit in all its created ordinariness – God does not go beyond the normal processes of life unnecessarily, and we need not be more holy than the Divine. If we have agreed to read one of the Advices in Meeting, if the Charity Commission recommend that we should prepare an annual report in a particular format, if we have made a mental resolve to start each day with 15 minutes of yoga stretches, we don't need to look for a leading as well.

On a communal level, if we as humans can see that something is right and something else wrong, again we do not need a special leading. The Ten Commandments and Jesus' summary of the law into two commandments – "love God", "love your neighbour as yourself" – are a basic part of our routine discernment about how we live our daily lives.

For some of us this does not seem sufficiently religious. I remember an outburst in Meeting for Sufferings, when Friends felt that Britain Yearly Meeting was becoming "just a well-run charity". "I don't want to be part of a well-run charity, I want to be part of a religious group, a church," said a weighty Friend. The point is that we need to be an ordinary well-run organisation, with good structures and sensible practices, which we then make extraordinary by transcending, not discarding them.

What kind of God do we find?

What concept or image of God does this collective experience bring us to? For me, it implies a God who respects our personalities, our freedom and the processes of our lives, a Spirit who works in and through them but who can also suggest that we go beyond what we know, that we take part with the Spirit in the "new thing", the re-creation of the world in big and small ways. Ultimately this implies that God delights in us as we live "answerable to the design of our creation" including all the fullness of our own creativity.

It seems to me that God simultaneously *respects* the processes of our life and nature, and *is* the very energy of those processes. We see this in the way the Quaker business method works. Our business meetings demonstrate the normal processes of group dynamics. If, for example, a local business meeting has gathered immediately after meeting for worship and has gone on for an unexpectedly long time, everyone gets hungry and irritable and we are unlikely to make a sensible decision. The wise and experienced meeting Clerk will not allow this scenario to develop, and the Spirit operates through the Clerk's good sense. A Clerk of Meeting for Sufferings once said, "When we talk about God's will, we sometimes imply that there is a correct answer to every question, and we have to go through this sort of séance to determine God's will, and there's this awkward character, God, who knows the answer, but for some reason won't tell us what it is. I think language about God's will is talking about the process not the answers, including the creative part. We come together not to discover God's will, but almost to create God's will, rather than to find it – it's a creative discovery process. If we see it as a creative thing, we have a contribution to make, a role in creating it."

If God acts in this way, there is a definite paradox in the open and yet hidden way this all seems to work. We are not dealing here with esoteric mysteries, the key of which is only given to initiates. The Spirit prefers to act through ordinary people, with their consent and co-operation, using their individual gifts and natures. The world is such that God can be in it and disappear into it, but God is not just hidden in creation – God is beyond and transcends the universe.

The Spirit, the Divine, is hidden, fluid, elusive, invisible like the wind, soft like breath, everywhere, like the atmosphere – the uncageable bird of heaven, the living flame, the water flowing through our grasp. We seem to see the Divine out of the corner of our eye; God leaves traces, a faint scent, a recognisable impression, a remembered style. "He's not like a tame lion."

The divine impulse moves, and moves us, towards the good, to peace, beauty, the best we can aspire to. All knowledge, all technology, is available to be used in the service of the good, under our consenting direction and if we co-operate with understanding and discernment, with each other and the inspiring Breath. We see the Spirit at work most clearly between people, in relationships and in communities, as we do things together, as we breathe the revivifying atmosphere of love together, in conspiracy with the divine impulse to healing and to re-creation. Using the principle that the Divine cannot be less than the highest of which we can conceive, we can look at those people whom we consider to be disciples of the Spirit, and who work for justice and for the world's healing, and we can interpret what they do as simultaneously their action and the Spirit's action moving towards the good of the world. In particular, Jesus' life, teaching, death and resurrection are a clear demonstration – for some the supreme example – of God's initiative and action in this world.

Our experience is of a God who acts, in the lives of individual people, in communities and in the world. The active verbs we use – God acts, God intervenes – are metaphorical but also profoundly truthful. There is a strong element in the Christian tradition, going back to Jesus, which speaks of God in personal terms while recognising that this does not limit the Divine to the personal. Speaking of God as a person does not reduce God to being a person.

What of the nature of God in Godself? Here again I can only speak for myself about what I have worked out; each of us, in and outside the Quaker community, has to work this out for ourself and then live by the result. But of course we borrow each other's words, and we begin with a caution from Thomas Aquinas, who reminds us that God is not a thing alongside other things to be examined. The Divine, the ground of being, is of a different order. In Isaac Penington's words, "God is the fountain of beings and natures, the inward substance of all that appears" (*Some Questions and Answers*, 1662, in Penington, 2005).

I put this into my simplistic understanding of scientific terms, and I guess that for me, the Divine is energy, energy as the inward substance of everything, apparently motionless in visible objects like a table, or a glass of water, but mobile in radio waves and in our thoughts. This links with the understanding of God as the Ground of our Being, as the creator and sustainer of the universe.

And where is this God?

But what does all this about "energy" and "the inward substance of all that appears" mean for us as individuals, as people? It sounds very impersonal, and among the root questions for each of us are, "Can I look positively on the universe? Is the universe positive towards me?" As the philosopher John Macquarrie put it, "Is Being gracious?"

Each of us can receive Good and recognise it as good, as fit and right for us. The hungry person, given food, knows that it's what they need and can take it in and be nourished; the unloved person, given love, can recognise it and grow with it. When we are starving for love or for food, we need it to be given skilfully so that our bodies and hearts can assimilate it, but this is how our deepest nature is made – our nature, our creation, is such that we are made to grow and to flourish. The inward substance of everything is the creative fountain of beings and natures.

Creation in time implies finitude; the flowers on the meeting house table wither and die, as do we; when we accept and receive creation as a gift in time we accept its ending. Creation is limited by being in time, while God is beyond time. Being in time ourselves, we see the eternal through the temporal. The eternal holds the temporal; eternity encloses time. Imagine the musical notes of a tune. We hear the notes one after the other, in time, but because we know the tune, we can hold the whole sequence of the tune in our head and hear it as a whole, beyond the immediate sequence. An experienced musician can step outside time and grasp the whole of a piece of music in this way. Can we imagine God holding all the temporal sequence of the moments of our life in one whole, in eternity? And thus seeing our life as a whole? Remembering that according to physicists, time is not in any case an absolute.

Can I also suggest that God, being outside and beyond time and space, chooses to create within time and space, and thus limits God's Godness? God is intimately involved in creation, as the conscious stuff of all energy and matter, and as the impulse of love, creativity, all good and all beauty. This creation is totally knowable and discoverable by the beings in it, and includes conscious human beings, who can choose to relate harmoniously to the Divine or to create ultimate disharmony. So the process of creation limits God.

We just do not know about God's relationship with other parts of the universe, with whatever consciousness may exist in the Champagne Supernova or the Pole Star – but we can expect surprises. And in the Christian myth, God becoming human means the source of creativity accepting the limits and finitude of creation.

The poetic language of our Christmas carols stretches and breaks with this paradox of incarnation:

> Behold, the great Creator makes
> Himself a house of clay
>
> . . .
>
> Hark, hark, the wise eternal Word
> Like a weak infant cries.
>
> (*The English Hymnal* no. 23)

Jesus of Nazareth in particular lived and spoke as a person closely in touch with the Spirit and in full co-operation with God. Jesus enables us to think of God in concrete form. His insights, words and way of being inspire me; they provoke me to reflection and action. Above all, he lived out his own words about bringing more abundant life – especially to people who were poor and marginalised, who sensed that "God is with us in this man". He expected and received hostility from the people and organisations to whom this God-centred life was threatening; he lived by his values and convictions to the point of being executed by the system as a result. Many of the things Jesus said and did have started shifts of attitude leading to huge movements and changes within the human community on this planet. His challenging insights into people's natures continue to resonate and have effects in our behaviour and thinking. This is where I see the Divine at work, in the sparks of power and illumination which help us to grow and move us all forward.

One of the biggest inner changes came about because of Jesus' death and the discovery that he was still very much alive after it. His friends had an overwhelming conviction that the God whom they knew through their Jewish tradition, and whom Jesus had shown them in his life, was acting most powerfully both in Jesus' powerless death and in his renewed presence with them. Many of their own lives were radically and dramatically changed as a result, even more than by their earlier friendship with him, as they lived with the powerful daily leadings of the Spirit, and tried to make sense of their discoveries and experiences together.

I see in the story of Jesus a clear example of God acting in the world, giving us a leading, showing energy working for good and asking for our co-operation, asking us to work alongside the Spirit. In the two thousand year story of the friends of Jesus, we all see plenty of twisted motives and horrors, subtle or unsubtle, crushing the human spirit; and we see these in the story of our own Society, too. But always we see resurrection popping up again. A new generation, a new chance, a new opportunity is offered us, to work with the good power, and to grow once more.

And where was God in all this human experience? Was Jesus' life and death just a great human example or was God there, in all the human reactions, failure, recovery and forgiveness, transformation and new growth? If God is involved in all creation, then God is thoroughly involved in Jesus, who lived because of God's initiative – a human being in total accord and co-operation with the divine Spirit and the Spirit's loving purposes.

I am convinced that the elusive breath, the energy which flows through the universe, wants to be in touch, wants us to be in touch, to love each other and to flow in the love which pours through everything. This gives us genuine hope, rooted and grounded in reality, in what C.S. Lewis calls "deeper magic from before the dawn of time"

(Lewis, 1987, p.142); it is true in eternity. I define love as a will for the loved ones' good together with a respect for their being. The Greek word *agapé* is often used in this sense, and Oliver Postgate summed it up for me in his poem entitled "Agapé", another piece of my mental furniture:

> I will not lumber you with love,
> nor climb on you to measure you for sins,
> nor wipe you over with forgivenesses,
> nor kick your shins.
> I know your eyes do not see out of mine,
> nor are your tears the tears I shed.
> But I don't care,
> for I will take your hand and make a place for you
> because you're there.
> Not for some complicated ploy
> of pity, piety or private greeds,
> but for that older simpler joy
> that, nothing wanting, nothing needs,
> except to live.
> For as I see you feel the rain
> and breathe the air,
> so just to know the sun that shines on you
> shines on me too
> confirms the sunlight,
> makes it sure,
> tells us we live, are there,
> that now will do,
> and asks no more.

5. The Mess of Creation

Finitude, freedom and evil

So far, everything in the garden is lovely, and we might echo the triumphant words of George Fox in 1647: "When God doth work, who shall let [i.e. hinder] it?" (*QF&P* 19.02). As he found out and as we know, a lot of things can hinder the work of God. Does this imply a God who is not omnipotent? What about the flaws in creation, the flaws in ourselves, and the times we have wilfully made a real mess of things? How does this reality fit with an understanding of creation?

God, just by creating something which is other than God, limits God's own potential and cuts off all sorts of possibilities. One classic way of putting this is to say that God cannot create a square circle, because the essence of circles is their circleness and that rules out squareness. But this is only a problem if our definition of God is the God of Greek philosophy, a God who is all-powerful. This is such an implicit "given" in many people's understanding of the Divine that if we shake in any way the picture of an all-powerful God, it feels to some as if we are taking away their whole concept of God.

Why do we automatically think that omnipotence is a necessary part of our concept of the Divine? It is an attractive image, expressed in much traditional teaching; it's worth looking at where the idea came from, and the experience that lies behind it. We older Friends probably learnt it from a variety of hymns in school; maybe younger Friends are not so burdened by it. The concept was developed by the fourth-century Greek philosophers and is not part of the Hebrew understanding of God; it is largely theoretical, appealing to us in the same way as it is appealing to think that our parents, or the legal system or the State, or the Society of Friends or the United Nations, can step in and set everything right. When put as simply as this, it is obvious, painfully, that life is just not like that. We have, in Bonhoeffer's phrase, come of age; we cannot get out of our responsibilities by handing them over to a parent figure (see p.81).

Because the universe is created, is here, and is consistent in its being, God's infinite potential is voluntarily and necessarily limited.

The colours of the rainbow follow each other in their sequence because that is the nature of things, in all the depth which that phrase implies. Creation therefore necessarily implies limits and finitude – there is a point at which the blue in the rainbow stops and the green begins; the life of any one created thing is limited, whether it is a human being or the sun; and time itself, as a dimension of creation, is also limited. We see the limitations of creation in earthquakes, tsunamis, our cats catching pigeons and us eating meat – all that is part of the tragic finitude of the world.

We too are part of this universe, and can look at it and reflect on it and choose to change it, in co-operation with the nature of things. We can change the genes of the flowers on our meeting house table, and develop a blue rose. We cannot change the spectrum of the rainbow. We hear echoes here of Woolman's suggestion that either we live according to the design of our creation – or we can choose otherwise: we can choose to live against our own design and that of creation and take the consequences, individually and communally. The energy of creation puts itself in our hands. "All that is", the universe, is open-ended – still in process, still evolving – the energy is still streaming and we can share in the creation of new things. We are invited to choose – God leaves us free to work with the grain of the universe, or to mess it up.

We see this pattern in the Gospels, too. Jesus invited people to join a community of abundant life, and people refused for a variety of reasons: "I have bought a field, I have married a wife, I have a new car, I am in a new relationship" (Luke 14:16–20). We have the chance to help those who are lying by the side of the road, beaten up by various things that have come upon them – or we can choose to pass by on the other side, hurrying to our religious work or our constitutional discussions.

And sometimes – often – we consciously will the bad, we say the hurtful words, we wilfully shatter the new creation, and when our wrongness becomes obvious, we add to it by denying the truth. We get enmeshed in a destructive cycle, individually and together, as communities, as nations, as the whole human race. Friends often avoid looking at this; we hasten to say that there is that of God in everyone. Yet as we look at the world with integrity and truth and as we work to put some things right, we are obliged to accept that some things in creation are twisted, that people turn to evil, that systems are corrupted, that as well as the seed of God, there is also the potential for badness in all of us.

As our outreach develops we must find a way of talking about this without abandoning our essentially positive and hopeful starting point. Seekers are not drawn to rose-coloured visions of a perfect human society; they know too much about life as it really is. London Friends, talking with hundreds of interested enquirers on Monday nights at Quaker Quest, found that after publishing three books on Quaker views of God, worship and peace, they were obliged to produce *Twelve Quakers and Evil* because the newcomers demanded that we should face the issue. As we consider the rational grounds for our understanding of God, how do we deal with this potential and actual reality of twisting, of wrongdoing in us, in others and in creation?

Renewal of life

Let us consider the experience and words of James Nayler, an early Quaker leader. After the awful stress of a six-week trial for blasphemy before Parliament, a brutal punishment and the breakdown of his relationship with other leading Friends, Nayler collapsed. Gradually recovering, he reflected on his experience. He lived close to God during that time of anguish and recovery, physical and mental, and as he later lay dying from a savage beating-up, he dictated his final testament, saying, "Let this be written for those that come after . . . There is a spirit which I feel, that delights to do no evil, nor to revenge any wrong . . . " (QF&P 19.12). His experience of God does not just underlie these words, it blazes from them. In the middle of this passage is a key sentence which we often do not notice among the beautiful cadences. He writes of this Spirit, which was in him and yet not only him: "its ground and spring is the mercies and forgiveness of God." James Nayler discovered not only a solid foundation – the "ground" of this spirit – but also the fountain of new life, the "spring" which flows from the ground. Both the ground and the spring, he testified – both the foundation and the fountain – are the mercies and forgiveness of God.

Nayler reflected on and used the biblical word "mercy", which is rooted in the Hebrew *chesed*, the committed love of God, promised and reliable. This is a deeper concept than the idea of "stretching a point to let someone off a due punishment". Translating *chesed* into English, people use a cluster of phrases: "steadfast love", "covenanted mercies" or, in Isaiah 55:3, " . . . an everlasting covenant, my steadfast sure love . . . " This is all more personal, more dynamic, more involved than the Greek philosophers' "omnipotence". By using the plural "mercies" rather than the singular "mercy", Nayler suggests that for him this is more than simply a part of God's character; he implies that there were several times in his life when God's mercy, God's solid loving presence, was a definite personal experience. He describes these occasions more fully in the passage we now have in *Quaker Faith & Practice* 20.21.

God's mercy in this sense, God's committed love, is surely one of the solid foundations of our silence, and a spring, an up-welling source, a creative resilience, within our hearts and meetings, and in our work for peace and justice.

James Nayler also experienced God's forgiveness. He was tried, then brutally punished by the State, for a thoughtless action which also led to a difficult falling-out within the early Quaker community. He realised his mistake and publicly admitted it, but it was hard to repair the friendships. William Dewsbury, one of the first Quaker mediators, helped both sides with this. In our communities, in our meetings and in society at large, we can mediate God's forgiveness. We all share the power of the keys, the power of locking people into hell or opening up heaven; in our Quaker understanding this power of forgiveness is given to all of us. It is not restricted to the clergy. We can shut people out of the community of friendship, and exclude them because of real or imagined mistakes; or we can re-create our community, unlock the fountains and springs of love and let new life flow.

In the media, we sometimes see an individual who forgives an appalling wrong – rape, or the murder of a child – and we wonder what greatness of soul, what faith is needed to do this; we ask ourselves if we could do the same. We can all tell other less public stories from our own experience. We know that this forgiveness isn't simple or easy, whether from the divine or from the human angle. Forgiveness isn't a sticking plaster we can put on the outside of a wound, it's an inner event, a process of healing from within, at depth. Sometimes the wound has to be re-opened to be cleansed, with loving and patient skill. Often we deny that the wound is there, so truth-telling, integrity, is part of the healing; and we need the skills, wisdom and expertise of conflict resolution, of counselling, of psychiatry, of friendship.

Jesus reminded us that to receive forgiveness ourselves, we
also need to be forgiving (Matthew 6:14–15; Matthew 18:21–35). We
sometimes find it hard to accept that others have been forgiven. In
Jesus' story of the welcoming father and the spendthrift son (Luke
15:11–32) we may recognise ourselves in the law-abiding and frugal
elder brother, who today would surely be a weighty member of his
meeting. Our capacity for forgiveness can grow, but for some of us
this growth is very difficult. The wound is too deep, too maiming, the
mental scar tissue is too strong. We hope that our inner re-creative
resilience can start from where we are; the disabling past can become
the ground from which the spring can come.

Bringing darkness to light

Is it possible to take an imaginative spiritual leap and to see the Spirit's
repairing work in loving and creative human responses to terrible
individual human actions? And in the way people respond to even
more terrible mass horrors planned and carried out by us human
beings – the Holocaust, the Rwandan genocide, the Middle East wars,
the London bombings in July 2005 and countless others in history
– and the awful persistence of torture and child abuse? We could make
a long list – but if we are searching for God at work in these actions
and reactions, it is good to remember the fruit of Nayler's experience:
"Art thou in the Darkness? Mind it not, for if thou dost it will fill thee
more . . . wait in patience till Light arises out of Darkness to lead
thee . . . " (QF&P 21.65).

Paul of Tarsus wrote about this complex interweaving of God's
dynamic righteousness and our tendency and compulsion to turn
aside, to fail in what we are trying to do. In his letter to the Roman
Christians, he theorises for several chapters and eventually is driven
to describe the personal experience which underlies his theories. He
has to be personal: "Wanting what's good, it seems, comes naturally,
but doing it does not. So I don't do the good thing I intend; instead,
the bad thing I want to avoid is what I do . . . Sin, *wishing to look like
sin*, used goodness to do the work of death in me, so that sin might
reach the height of sinfulness" (Romans 7:13–19, Gaus' translation;
my italics). The NRSV translation puts the italicised words slightly
differently: ". . . in order that sin might be shown to be sin". The
wrongness of the crusades, the bombing of Dresden, my shouting at

my children when I can't stand any more, is visible; a hidden tendency to rottenness is brought into the Light and is openly shown to be bad, and now that it is in plain sight it can be dealt with. Again visibility and light are the metaphors. Using this visual and contemplative imagery, could it be that part of the way God works with the human tendency to badness is to intensify it, to bring it to a head, to bring it into the Light? Because of the media, we see so much more now of the effects of war and evil in the wider world. Jesus was crucified in full public view. Do we have to see, to acknowledge, our addiction to doing wrong things?

Others may wish to use another set of images: this is my personal understanding. But as Friends we need to work out a rationale of evil for ourselves, individually and together, and our own individual statements of belief must include some thought on this. We cannot just disregard its existence. The experience and thinking of Quakers who deal daily with marred creation and its effects would be really valuable here to the rest of the Society.

I cherish and have often reflected on two sentences from a colleague. In his peace work he often went to meet people deeply enmeshed in the twisted structures of a powerful state, and he commented to me: "It's no good making the outward journey to meet people who are doing these terrible things unless you first make the inward journey to meet that of God in them." Later he spoke of the anguish of the death of his son in a car accident: "I use the words of Jacob wrestling with the angel, 'I will not let you go unless you bless me' (Genesis 32:26). I try to find a blessing in his innocent pointless suffering and death." We need to think and write more about these elements of our human and Quaker experience. If God is God, and if our understanding of God is big enough, there is Light to arise out of this darkness.

6. Expressing our Faith

No fixed crystal

When Quakers talk about statements of belief, we usually say that we prefer to think of Truth as a growing and developing understanding, rather than as a final statement backed by the authority of our religious group and used as a test for membership. "Truth . . . is a seed with the power of growth, not a fixed crystal, be its facets never so beautiful" (J.W. Rowntree, *QF&P* 27.21). Our preferred method with words about religious experience, thinking and belief is to collect different people's experiences and reflections, so *Quaker Faith & Practice*, our Book of Discipline, takes the form of an anthology. It is authoritative in the sense that we have all agreed in Yearly Meeting to accept it as normative for us at this time, but we know that it has changed and developed in the past and we look forward to its development in the future. We do not use it as a test for any individual's membership, though we want members to know what is in it and to feel comfortable with it.

It is interesting that the broad outline of the method we use to re-create it resembles that used by the early Church as the Gospels and the rest of the New Testament came into being. The friends of Jesus found that some of the stories about him helped them to go on living together in this new way, so they repeated them to each other, and they also remembered and quoted to each other the things Jesus said which stuck in their minds because they continued to be inspiring and life-giving. Eventually they were written down, after being repeated for several decades by the community. In the same way, when as a community we re-create *Faith & Practice*, we ask each other: "What Quaker words, new and old, have you remembered? What Quaker words continue to be useful in your individual and corporate experience and in your lives, growth and practice?"

Perhaps an individual Quaker, working through an addiction to smoking, has looked through the letters of George Fox and found that his words leap off the page: "Whatever ye are addicted to, the tempter will come in that thing" (*QF&P* 20.42). Or one treasurer faced with a difficult problem asks for guidance, and another replies, "I found what the Annual Conference of Treasurers minuted six years ago really useful; I'll send you the wording." Often a clerk, after several months of hard work on a tricky issue, says, "That's why that section is in *Faith & Practice* – now I see what it means." Or the experienced Friends House administrator, accustomed to responding to anxious telephone calls, keeps a marker in their desk copy of *QF&P* at paragraph 4.20, which urges Friends to avoid legal actions between themselves, and also keeps handy George Fox's advice to Elizabeth Claypole in her depression, "Be still and cool . . .", the essence of which is, "Don't look at your sins, but at the Light which shows them up" (*QF&P* 2.18). Many of the words in *Faith & Practice* are not credal statements but working tools.

So are the Gospels and much of the New Testament. The "Jesus Community" in first-century Palestine had a lot to do with the occupying Roman army, and some of the soldiers found the new Community attractive – so the stories of Jesus' conversation with the friendly Roman centurion were remembered and re-told (Luke 7:1–10). Relationships with unfriendly Romans were not so easy – so people reminded each other of Jesus' words about being compelled to carry the soldier's pack for one mile, and going the extra mile too (Matthew 5:41). The women in the new community were determined to hold on to the equal recognition Jesus had given them, so they made sure that several stories about them were re-told, as well as Jesus' words about children. The whole community found that life was often turbulent – so every one of the four strands of tradition caught in the canonical Gospels includes the story of the little boat tossed up and down in the storm on the Lake of Galilee, and the calming words and presence of Jesus (Matthew 8:23–27; Mark 4:36–41; Luke 8:22–25; John 6:16–21). I realised that I could trust the accuracy of much of the Gospel accounts of Jesus' words when I found myself re-telling stories that my Quaker teacher Harold Loukes had told me 40 years previously, when I studied under him in Oxford; he made such an impression that I use the exact words he used, and often the exact intonation.

Similarly, the letters written to the small communities of "The Way" were kept because they were useful records of advice and experience, worth the shelf space and worth copying. The Book of Revelation, which causes people so many headaches but which was valued and endlessly quoted by the first Quakers, is actually a politico-religious pamphlet written in pictorial code, kept because it was inspiring and worth the shelf space in the first century. Walter Wink's *The Powers* trilogy (Wink, 1984, 1992, 1993) helps us to get to grips with Revelation and to understand the experience behind it; the writer himself tells us that it began as ministry in worship: "I was in the spirit on the Lord's Day" (Revelation 1:10), so perhaps we can take it with Advice 17: "When words are strange or disturbing to you, try to sense where they come from and what has nourished the lives of others."

So both *Faith & Practice* and the Gospels are foundations for faith, in the sense that they are rooted in the living experience and produced within the life of communities of faith, with the authority of the community and of the truth within the words.

What lies behind?

We Quakers also do something else very significant with words about God and about religious practice – we look through them, asking, "What experience lies behind this statement?" The Indian Chief Papunehang, after hearing John Woolman speak, said "I love to feel where words come from" (Woolman ed Moulton, 1971, p.133). Friends are practised in thus exploring for the source of words and language; we all do it in meeting for worship when we listen to ministry.

Our understanding of the Divine, of God, is the foundation of our actions and our thinking, of the way we choose to live and to worship. Even if we don't consciously formulate our understanding, it is there as a motive, as the basis, the root of our lives. Each of us has our own understanding of God, created consciously or not out of our own experiences, starting before our birth, and out of our own emotional and intellectual history. We share some elements of it with others, while other elements are unique to us.

Our understanding of God is like a big house in which we have been born and which we explore as we grow. We make ideas and pictures with the materials we find in it, we bring lots of things in from outside, we find some interesting things in its library, we cook other things up for ourselves in its kitchen, and we make our own music and pictures. Sometimes things in the cellar burst through and surprise us, sometimes we rummage in the attic and find an old concept which we re-make into something useful. Meeting for worship is one place where we turn over the pictures, re-play the video

clips and connect the ideas. Talking with others is another chance
to look at our understandings together and to learn from each other.
Living by our ideas is where we really test them out in practice. What
happens if I follow this leading? Is there that of God in everyone? Does
nonviolence work?

It's useful to be aware of the imagery and metaphor which is often
hidden in the words we use and which other Friends use. We Quakers
love the picture language of metaphor – our classic two are the slightly
abstract metaphor of Light, and the more organic one of Seed and
growth. Listen to ministry in meeting for worship and see how often
it is given in a variety of metaphorical forms. Our concern for truth
asks us to appreciate and enjoy the metaphors but also to look behind
them, grasping what is being said and perhaps recasting it in our own
picture language, often a language or a way into experience which is
personal to us as individuals.

> All Truth is a shadow, except the last, except the utmost;
> yet every Truth is true in its kind. It is substance in its own
> place, though it be but a shadow in another place (for it is but
> a reflection from an intenser substance); and the shadow is
> a true shadow, as the substance is a true substance.
>
> *QF&P* 27.22

Using the language of Light, Isaac Penington wrote this in
1653 during his platonist period before he became a Friend, but we
recognise it as true to our experience. Can we push deeper for the
Truth behind our careful language, and will we find a unifying truth, or
a divisive one?

I find that my natural metaphors are often words about building,
solidity and foundations, words which imply a rather planned and
organised approach. Having been involved in Quaker fundraising
for several years I know that the way we talk about Quaker money is
often a way of metaphorically talking about the Society's energy. In
ministry, some of us may use words mostly about air and clouds and
sky – a different approach; neither is better or worse, they are just part
of that person's experience, of "where the words come from".

A classic example illustrating how we can grasp whence the words
come and how we mix imagery with experience comes from Luke

Cock's talk to a Quaker gathering in 1721; he used the crossroads in Shrewsbury, the Weeping Cross, as the image of the development of his faithful discipleship:

> Necessity, Friends, outstrips the law: necessity has made many go by the Weeping Cross . . . I remember I was yonce travelling through Shrewsbury, and my Guide said to me: "I'll show thee the Weeping Cross." "Nay," said I, "thou need not; I have borne it a great while." Now this place that he showed me was four lane ends.
>
> I remember when I first met with my Guide. He led me into a very large and cross [place], where I was to speak the truth from my heart – and before I used to swear and lie too for gain. "Nay, then," said I to my Guide, "I mun leave Thee here: if Thou leads me up that lane, I can never follow: I'se be ruined of this butchering trade, if I mun't lie for gain." Here I left my Guide, and was filled with sorrow, and went back to the Weeping Cross: and I said, if I could find my good Guide again, I'll follow Him, lead me whither He will. So here I found my Guide again, and began to follow Him up this lane and tell the truth from my heart. I had been nought but beggary and poverty before; and now I began to thrive at my trade, and got to the end of this lane, though with some difficulty.
>
> But now my Guide began to lead me up another lane, harder than the first, which was to bear my testimony in using the plain language. This was very hard; yet I said to my Guide, "Take my feeble pace, and I'll follow Thee as fast as I can. Don't outstretch me, I pray Thee." So by degrees I got up here.
>
> But now I was led up the third lane: it was harder still, to bear my testimony against tithes – my wife not being convinced. I said to my Guide, "Nay, I doubt I never can follow up here: but don't leave me: take my pace, I pray Thee, for I mun rest me." So I tarried here a great while, till my wife cried, "We'se all be ruined: what is thee ganging stark mad to follow t'silly Quakers?" Here I struggled and cried, and begged of my Guide to stay and take my pace: and presently my wife was convinced. "Well," says she, "now follow thy

Guide, let come what will. The Lord hath done abundance for us: we will trust in Him." Nay, now, I thought, I'll to my Guide again, now go on, I'll follow Thee truly; so I got to the end of this lane cheerfully . . .

My Guide led me up another lane, more difficult than any of the former, which was to bear testimony to that Hand that had done all this for me. This was a hard one: I thought I must never have seen the end of it. I was 11 years all but one month in it. Here I began to go on my knees and to creep under the hedges, a trade I never forgot since, nor I hope never shall. I would fain think it is unpossible for me to fall now, but let him that thinks he stands take heed lest he fall.

QF&P 20.22

The language is Luke Cock's own, yet the experience behind the image is clear and commentary on the passage is unnecessary; it just sits like a great rock of experience in our Book of Discipline. We cannot deny the authority of his testimony, nor ask him to change his language just because it is not ours.

We also enter someone else's inner experience when we sing – perhaps the Leaveners' songs or the hymns of another tradition, of whatever faith. As we enter into the music as well as the words, we are entering the creative worshipful meditation of the composer and the writer on the mystery they are bringing to us, we are sharing someone else's experience of where the words come from, and making it our own. And maybe we are moved to re-create it, to re-write it closer to our own vision, to set the words to a new tune, or to re-write the words so that they express our own feelings.

In interchurch and interfaith relationships, when we are trying to see another group's faith from their point of view, it's useful to ask again, "What experience underlies these words?" even if only in our own minds. When we share in worship with another faith or church it's often easier to grasp the inner meaning of their words and teaching, because we are actually doing things together rather than theorising. This happens both ways. I recall arranging a meeting for worship for delegates to a Churches Together in Britain and Ireland gathering; we started with the hymn to the Holy Spirit, "Come, Holy Ghost, our souls inspire", which many of the clergy there would have sung at their ordination as priests. Two or three people, non-Quakers who were accustomed to Quaker worship, ministered in a deep silence, and afterwards one Catholic representative who had been trying to understand us for many years said, "Now I see what you are talking about, I see how it works." Similarly, standing at the back during worship in the glorious Hindu Mandir in Neasden, I caught a glimpse in people's faces of the meaning of offering actual food to the elaborate statues of the Hindu gods.

This does not mean that we necessarily agree with what we are watching or assent to all the teaching, but we understand our fellow human beings better, and their relationship with God. I recall the face of a priest I knew years ago. He was a fervent Anglo-Catholic, the secretary of the Society of King Charles the Martyr, and when he preached about the place of women I wanted to get up on the pew like George Fox and shout back at him. But one Maundy Thursday evening he carried the blessed sacrament in procession, with candles and incense, to the Altar of Repose. His face shone with devotion, love, reverence and awe. We didn't ever discuss his thinking or my thinking – I was too timid at that time – but I understood then something of the experience which lay behind his ideas.

Beyond experience: Quakers and theology

In our reflection on religious and spiritual concepts, we value experience highly, and we quote George Fox's words, "This I knew experimentally" (QF&P 19.02). This is fundamental to our thinking. When we talk over our individual and corporate understanding of God, it is helpful to start from our experiences, both shared and separate; in this way we earth the discussion, and link our heads with our hearts and our bodies.

There are, however, some limits to basing everything on experience. Many of us learnt our first mathematics by setting out three bricks or apples or conkers, and adding two more to them, counting them and saying, "Now there are five!" And perhaps we went further and added a second row of five bricks and realised that twice five, when we count them all, makes ten. This is experiential mathematics. Much of the maths we did in school could be experienced in concrete form, and there is a practical usefulness in this. To build Chartres Cathedral, or the large meeting house in Friends House, demanded a level of applied mathematics and engineering knowledge which may be graspable in the same way as our minds grasp adding up our bricks. But we don't stay at this primary, immediately concrete level; it is possible to go on to more advanced mathematics and highly-developed engineering, both for the creativity of abstract thought and to achieve practically useful things, such as buildings which can withstand earthquakes, or tsunami warning systems, or an understanding of weather and climate.

In maths, I reached the level of differential calculus, and my mind just couldn't go any further. But when someone who knows about it tells me that according to the scientific community's studies of climate change, this or that is likely to happen and this is the action I need to take, I assess their credentials and then trust their expertise; I don't say, "Before I believe you, I have to follow every single step of your reasoning and be able to grasp it myself."

So with theological and philosophical study. Theology, "words about God", and philosophy, "the love of wisdom", can both be practical and helpful as well as inspiring and beautiful in themselves. And doing Quaker theology means not just discussion, but worship, action, work, business – so, actually, we all do it. Quaker theologians, a growing group, enjoy playing in the presence of God, working with their technical concepts – holiness, love, creation, faith, humility, ecclesiology – and they hope to produce words, at the deepest level ministry, which are useful to the rest of us and help us to come closer to the Divine. Theology is not just a personal hobby, it's done on behalf of a community. As individuals, we can work out our own thinking based on our personal experience, and when we need to say something together about God we can ask our theologians to work it out, grounding their words in our shared experience – and this too can be a collaboration in which we work with the Spirit.

So the question "What experience lies behind these words?" is valuable, but it has limitations. And as we learn to put these pointed questions to people in the other churches and faiths, we will also hear their equally penetrating questions to us:

"How do you articulate authority?"
"Where does the teaching come in?"
"Why is it all so vague?"

"Why is it all in pamphlets, not books?"

"How do you live and keep centred with just one hour's silent meditation each week?"

We say we have a lot to offer the other churches – as we offer our riches, we often have to explain them, and learn about them as we tell others.

It's not difficult for us to enter in at some level to the experience of another faith, when we visit temples or sit in the church of another denomination. Some of us enjoy going to Quaker meetings across the world where the worship is Quaker but excitingly different: for instance, where Friends sing to guitar accompaniment but still hold the peace testimony. However, it's far more difficult to sit in our own meeting house in Britain and to listen to another British Quaker minister in words which offend us, which we find hurtful.

There are two groups of British Quakers who can hurt other Friends badly by their ministry, and both groups are then hurt themselves by the response of others. I have heard ministry from those of us who have gone beyond Christian language and concepts, and who cheerfully leap beyond theism and God-language; these Quakers sometimes speak as if other Friends are immature and will one day grow out of their childish dependence on old-fashioned imagery. On the other hand, I have also heard ministry from those of us who have a close and precious relationship with Jesus, God and the Spirit; these Quakers sometimes speak as if everyone else simply has to turn to the Christian God to be flooded with the experience of God's love. Friends speak in bewildered hurt – or in fury – of being eldered for both these sorts of ministry, and we probably all know of meeting communities which have been deeply divided by reactions to it. As we disagree, we can learn three things to enable our communities to be gathered rather than divided.

Firstly, we can ask our question: "What experience lies behind these words?" This demands a certain distancing, an abstract examination which may not be immediately possible, but which cools the first heated response.

Secondly, we can recall an idea that J. S. Mill apparently developed from Coleridge, and which I find helpful in ecumenical discussion and Quaker discussion: "People are mostly right in what they affirm, and wrong in what they deny." So when I speak positively about my own experience of the greatness of, say, the music of Mozart, I am right, but if I say that "Groups like Oasis and Coldplay are complete rubbish, I can't see anything in their music, and what's more, I don't want anyone ever to mention their names in front of me", I am wrongly denying what is a positive experience for many people. In interchurch discussion, when Quakers affirm that "all of life is sacramental; the Divine can speak to us through everything in creation" we are right, and when we say that "the sacraments that the other churches use are utterly pointless mumbo-jumbo" we are denying the experience of many others. Theirs may not be a positive experience for us, but especially if our theology is based on experience, we cannot just wipe the experience of many other human beings off our mental map. In our meetings, can we ask ourselves, "What are the people whom we find so difficult denying, what are they affirming – and why? What am I denying, and what am I affirming – and why?" Can we search for what is positive in whatever has been said? For the time being, can we focus on that and let the rest go?

Thirdly, we can remind ourselves that in our free Quaker community we have some disciplines and inner restraints. If there is one quotation from *Faith & Practice* which I would carve over every meeting house door it is the words of Frederick Parker Rhodes: "What is forbidden me? . . . to despise another's wisdom, to blaspheme another's God" (*QF&P* 26.41).

At a later stage, not in ministry in that meeting for worship, and not immediately afterwards, can the meeting think through and examine the varying understandings of and approaches to the Divine which its members have?

Travelling documents

To help us as we work out our own understanding of the Divine, for some time now we've had a mental tool in Britain Yearly Meeting's toolkit, which could again be valuable. In 1976 our Friend Jocelyn Burnell suggested to us that we might each occasionally prepare what she called a "travelling document", a summary for each of us individually of our own understanding of God at this time. "We should be prepared," she said, "to share provisional beliefs, and help one another to explore." Part of Jocelyn's own travelling document now stands in *Faith & Practice* at 26.25; her words have gone through our own community's anthologising process and we have given them authority for our generation.

Some of us will prefer to express our current belief in music, or perhaps in dance; some of us might paint it or carve it or make it in clay. It's our inner truth given outward form through our own creativity. Calling these our "travelling documents" preserves the sense of provisionality, and reminds us that as we continue to develop our discipleship we go on journeying deeper into our experience, our understanding and our faith.

> Ah! The bird of heaven!
> Follow where the bird has gone;
> Ah! The bird of heaven!
> Keep on travelling on.

Some of the early Church's creeds were statements of belief like this, provisional individual statements which were then accepted by communities as normative, attempting to put into words experiences which were beyond words but which people were trying to put across, to express in the thought-forms of their time. The Christians of the early centuries were attempting to keep people's understanding of God at a big enough level, putting a marker beside some unfruitful paths which some had tried, but which experience showed led to inadequate understandings of the immensity of God and the greatness of God's initiative and action in the world. The use later made of the creeds, to fix belief and exclude some from membership, does not diminish their original function as "the latest restatement of our belief in modern dress and today's language" which they certainly were when first written down.

I hope we might, each of us as individuals, feel able to say what we believe without worrying that this will become a "credal statement". A travelling document is not a creed, it is something different. Friends who cannot use theistic language have formulated their "travelling documents" in several books, notably David Boulton's *Godless for God's Sake* (2006). Quakers who find my thinking and formulations too traditional and God-centred may find these books more helpful.

Let's listen to ourselves carefully as we talk about our beliefs, especially when we talk to enquirers. It's very easy to talk about our Quaker faith entirely in terms of what we don't have and what we don't think, because so many of us have come to Quakerism from more restrictive formulations of thought which we have put behind us. If our travelling document is couched entirely in negative language, our thinking actually depends on what we are rejecting, which is not a solid foundation. In this sort of theological discussion, another question is useful – "What concept of God does this statement imply?" – and if the concept is inadequate, Friends and many others seriously doubt the validity of the assertion. If we say to a modern thinker in a more traditional church, "I can't believe in a God who sends people to Hell," we are quite likely to get the reply, "The God whom you don't believe in, I don't believe in either." We serve the truth best if we put our understanding in positive terms, as many Friends did in the Outreach pamphlet *This I Affirm* (QHS, 1999).

As we talk with those who come fresh to our meetings, they often ask us, "So what do you believe?" or "What do Quakers think about the mysteries of life and death?" We owe it to them to say something clear and understandable, so we have to make the effort first to put what we ourselves think into words. What we reject when we reject creeds is not rational thought, or the use of any words at all, but the use of words to imply or make explicit any sense that "because I believe this, you should believe it too", or "we all think this, so if you want to join us you must think it too". We have chosen as a corporate group to invite people to join, to be members, without testing their belief by a formula, and we have chosen to live without one single teaching authority; instead we invite each other to find and turn to our own inner authority, our own Inward Teacher in the words of early Quakers. There is nothing wrong with a thought-out belief; but the Quaker method is for each of us to think out our own or to hunt among our collection of the words of other Friends for something which fits our condition for the time being.

These personal provisional statements are the foundations, the building blocks, of our concept of God. We can borrow them from each other, or we can reject other people's words and draft our own. As we mature in faith, our own language changes, and the foundations we need also change. I find as I get older that I believe more and more in less and less. I find the essentials get stronger and more important – and for me the central thing is the love of God: that's what I put my faith in. But we each have to work it out for ourselves.

7. Living with Difference

What is your practice?

We started with Francis of Assisi's two questions: "God, who are you, and who am I?" We couldn't tackle the first question without also addressing the second; so we now have a partial answer to that query, "God, who am I?" We can ask this question corporately: "Who are we, we humans? Where did we come from? How can we be faithful disciples, answerable and faithful to the design of our creation, following and learning together? How are we human beings meant to work in relationship with the Divine?"

But a general answer isn't enough. Each of us asks for the answer to our own particular question, "Who am I, myself, in relation to God? How do I work with the rest of creation, and with my own divided and contradictory inner self? What is my own design? How can I live an inner life that is in integrity with my own individual nature?"

Let's start again with our experience. Rather than speculating about how we might develop and live out our relationship with the Divine, we can look at what we actually do and thus understand better who we are in relation to God, the nature of our discipleship in practice, and our development as religious beings, individually and collectively. Since this method starts from experience, rather than from theoretical notions, it is helpful to begin with some research.

In June 2005, I carried out a small survey asking people for their experience of what worked for them; it was limited in scope, but the answers were interesting. I put four questions to Friends and others, asking which disciplines helped them to keep their inner life centred and on track. By "discipline", I meant "an activity or a practice, maybe physical, maybe mental, which you try to make habitual and to do regularly even if you feel a bit reluctant – as a marathon runner has a discipline of running even on a pouring wet January morning".

The questions were these:

- What practice or discipline helps you to keep yourself, heart and soul, at your most loving and open to the Spirit?

- How has this practice and discipline developed during the course of your life?
- Is your practice shared with others?
- How does this sharing make a difference?

I also asked an extra question for those with small children: "How do you establish and keep to any sort of inner spiritual framework for your life?" People caring for small children really need some practical suggestions about how their situation can enrich rather than take away their inner life. Furthermore, the way we respond to a specific child and to the presence of children in our meetings, in our Society and in our daily lives, shows a great deal about our assumptions and our unconscious thinking. Children earth us and show us what really matters.

The survey asked for facts, not theory, for actual practical and effective actions, not prescriptions or suggestions or underlying principles, and the replies were fascinating. Some wrote of settled custom carried out over years, some of a practice they were trying to make habitual. One Friend in my own meeting isn't the sort of person who would write things down; he simply said, "People come first" – that is the sum of his spirituality and of his life. In all our exploration, it is good to balance what we say or write with how we visibly live our lives.

My research method was limited and coloured by the fact that the replies came from the sort of person who likes answering questionnaires and who can be articulate about their own inner life. We need also to recall another limitation which is shared not just by Friends but by practically the whole modern western Christian Church, and which affects us more widely than in our examination of these findings. People who are organised in their thinking are often also articulate and good with words, and systematic enough to get a book written and published. This means that most books about how to live an inner life are written by people who are coherent and precise, and they write about how they live their inner life – which is often word-based and highly organised. As a result, those of us who are far less articulate, and not so organised, read the books and feel in our guts that they don't speak to our condition. And so we feel marginalised. This understanding came to me as a great revelation and a great liberation. Apparently, we Quakers worship books as well as flowers and tables, and we need to hear – I certainly needed to hear – the corrective: that reading books about spirituality is not the only path to deepening our religious life. In fact, reading, and imagining that I am the sort of person I'm reading about, can be positively dangerous if I simply follow my fantasies.

Of those who did write down their thoughts, many said that doing something regularly is helpful; but we do different things. A regular time of quiet, often in the morning, suited half of the respondents, and John Woolman in the eighteenth century was just one of many Quakers throughout history who have kept up this solid tradition. Some of us call this meditation, others think of it as worship.

However, the Quaker tradition of grace before meals was only mentioned by a few Friends. This silent pause of thankfulness before we eat is an expression of our sacramental theology, and holds in being our conviction that every meal can be a way of linking ourselves with God. If we stop doing this, does this just mean that today's meals are more rushed and less shared, or have we lost our earlier conviction?

Many didn't even mention meeting for worship, just assuming it as a discipline. A younger Friend wrote:

Worship together strengthens, makes it easier somehow.
In another sense, sharing failure or distraction in prayer
with others, being open about it, is a source of strength.
Worship together is also a gentle kind of discipline: can I say
distractions are less distracting, have less purchase? There's
a holding, a keeping you there, that's more of a restraint on
"running off somewhere" than you get if alone.

In our daily practice, a few found physical exercise useful, whether it was swimming, aerobics, yoga, walking or running. It's interesting that all the non-Quaker respondents mentioned this, but several Friends also found value in the physical.

For many, taking part in demonstrations or vigils, working for peace or for the environment were essential; one Friend described this as "Putting my body where my beliefs are."

Some valued music not just in itself but as a regular centring practice: playing the piano alone, listening to Bach, singing or playing chamber music with others. One Friend, who said playing music was an essential for her, only recognised this after leaving it aside for three months. Another heard all these replies and commented wryly, "You can tell that this was a survey for Quakers, they're all Bach types!" What modern music – of any kind – do Friends find helpful?

Some said it was helpful to take part in the practice or liturgy of other denominations and other religions. Some mentioned going to Compline or to Buddhist meditation. It's worth noting what traditions seem to suit Quakers: some spoke of praying in the Celtic tradition, while others appreciated Benedictine liturgy and thought. Within the growth of Quaker thinking and practice in the last fifteen years, the Appleseed way of doing things has become a tradition which many Friends also appreciate (see Glossary).

Many Quakers can't do without writing, including journalling; one spoke of journalling in paint as well as words. For me, this illustrates the variety of what suits Quakers. I attended some Woodbrooke sessions on journalling partly because I reacted so strongly against the idea and thought that perhaps I was avoiding something I needed to look at. I learnt what it is, and that it isn't my way – so I can lay journalling aside. But it is a great Quaker tradition which we have found helpful over three and a half centuries. Many of the passages in *Quaker Faith & Practice* come from these journals, so present Friends' journalling is vital not "only" for their own sake, but for that of future Quakers.

We can hardly call practising laughter a discipline, but Friends value it; one Friend told me – and her face lit up as she said it – "I thank God for blessings, every day. Not necessarily at a set time, but I make sure I do."

Several respondents included praying for other people in their practice; one Friend did this while walking with her dog. She wrote,

> In the past few years I have developed a visualisation in which the sky becomes a great pavilion of light into which I bring people who are suffering. In my imagination they are warmed and illuminated by golden light. One friend is not brought inside because I know she would rather be free and unconfined, so I send her into the wind on the hilltops! These imaginings often lead to a resolve on some action.

The survey asked how people's practice had developed, and one replied,

> If a time machine could take me back, I would find my silence is different now. Certainly my confidence in it as a way of guidance, healing etc has grown enormously.

The question about children brought several insights. One Friend wrote,

> If there was something I wanted to think about, it was helpful to sign up to run a session about it for the children's class a few weeks hence. This gave me a period of time during which to focus on the issue, and a need to be able to say something really simple about it – or to base an activity for the children around it. Doing it this way meant that there wasn't really a tension between doing "my" thing and meeting the children's needs. It gave me a sort of discipline and framework within which to develop my spiritual life. Incidentally, it often led to some interesting discussions with both adults and children.

Quakers who work with our young people and children, as well as with enquirers, find they grow in the process, and learn a great deal too.

Several Friends took the opportunity to reflect on the whole idea of practice:

> There are many activities used to help in self-development, and I believe they all work – but only if you practise them. I have gradually come to realise that it is more important for me to be aware of what I find I *am* doing, rather than what might be of help *if* I were doing it.

> Using the simile of the marathon runner, you learn the discipline by doing it, the marathon runner runs.

> The idea of commitment is key. Commitment to family, to my music friends, to myself, to meeting through membership underpins the discipline.

We first find out what we want to be committed to, what for us is answerable to the design of our particular creation:

> There was a moment earlier this year when I felt so happy, balanced, calm and well that I looked at all the things I was doing at that time (diet, exercise, reading etc) and realised that these were the things I needed to do all the time in order to feel that good most of the time.

And finally, "What I do isn't so important, it's where it takes me, to stillness."

The responses showed a huge variety of actual practice, and one Friend spoke of "working with the rhythms of the day", which naturally vary for each of us, as do the rhythms of different periods in our lives. Some are evening people, others get up early; some use the journey to work as a time for reflection, others treasure the bedtime quiet with their children. For some, the intellectual stimulus of discussion is essential; another said, "My first spiritual experience was blockading the Greenham nuclear base"; another lay in a hammock, at one with the sun, the breeze and the birds. If we find it hard to accept all these as different ways of being Quakers, is this because we cannot be confident in our own path, our own way? Are we diminished in our own way of being if our neighbour has a different practice? In our community, how can we affirm each other's particular integrity and special discoveries?

We are all different, so we work out for ourselves different methods of keeping ourselves centred and on track. Some need a solid foundation of daily routine, others prefer to be grounded in the conviction that all our life is suffused with the Spirit, and find that this gives us a way of life with God which is anything but routine, and can vary hugely day by day and month by month.

In finding out and living by "what works for me", each of us is echoing John Woolman's "we live answerable to the design of our creation". The Quaker emphasis on integrity, on living by the truth about ourselves, is another way of putting the same insight. Many of the great teachers on spiritual development understood this. The Benedictine Abbot John Chapman (1865–1933) said simply: "Pray as you can, not as you cannot." When we live answerable to the design of our creation, we are really ourselves, we are energetic, radiant, fulfilled. It may not last, but we have been there and we know. Underlying this is a rediscovery of creation, in our spiritual practice, in our inner world, and in our deeper understanding of the ecological systems we share. George Fox said: "Each hath an office, and is serviceable" (Fox, 1698, Epistle 264) meaning that each Quaker has something particular of their own to contribute to the whole community.

Faithful discipleship means first finding my own integrity, the design of my creation, and then living by it, and moving on from that way of living when our life changes and a new way develops.

This small survey reaffirmed for me another discovery. At a time of crisis in the yearly meeting when the children of four families in Orkney were taken into care amid huge media publicity, I heard Friend after Friend say "What can we do? Well, we can pray about it", in a tone which implied this was a soundly tested resource, not a last desperate resort. I became aware then of an underground river of prayer which flows silently through the whole of Britain Yearly Meeting. I hope other Friends have discovered this when they needed it. The depth and insights of Quaker replies to this survey show that we know what we are talking about when we speak of the inner life, because we practise living with the Spirit day by day.

Knowing our "types"

In looking at how I am different from other people I have found a useful tool in the Jungian-based system, the Myers-Briggs Type Indicator, MBTI for short (for the Myers & Briggs Foundation, see www.myersbriggs.org). This is another example of a technical way of grasping our experience, and taking it further, in which people are sorted generally into 16 broad types, ranging from the person who is energised by engaging with other people, who is practical and physical and who follows what they feel, to the introverted person who tends to draw energy and meaning from within, who likes cool abstract thought and makes careful and judicious decisions. There are 14 other types between these two extremes. It is a tool to be used carefully; many Friends like it, though I know others find it positively unhelpful. The vital point is, there are a number of different psychological types of people, and what suits one of us does not suit another – and no one type of person is better or more acceptable than another. Some people are of the type who write and learn from reading; others of the type who act and learn from acting; some of us find refreshment in the tactile sensory arts such as cooking, weaving, or gardening; others in the more abstract arts of music or contemplation of great art.

For me, the great value of going through the MBTI process and finding my type was the confirming affirmation of me as what I am, the sense of recognition as I am described in my complexity. When I discovered my type I felt that I had found "the design of my creation" and could live better according to it. This affirmation can be very helpful, especially if you discover it alongside others who are finding the different design of their distinctive creation. MBTI practitioners are careful to stress the value of all the types of person. No one type is "better", "more worthy" or even "more quakerly" than any other. Other Friends prefer a different method, such as the Enneagram; the essential is the affirmation of your distinct personality, and the affirmation of the validity of difference.

It is a human weakness to use any system of classification of people as a means of putting other people down and affirming my own superiority: "Blonde Essex girls are dim", "People with university degrees are smarter", "Vegetarians are more moral than omnivores", "Quakers are superior types". We fall into this trap unconsciously, with our worst put-down: "that's not quakerly!" The inner reason for this tendency to classify and put down other people stems, I think, from a lack of confidence, fostered by our peculiar silent and unarticulated systems. Growing up as a Quaker child in this puzzling silent Quaker tribe, I learnt my way around by the unconscious signals given by other members of the meeting in their actions and tone of voice. I learnt some valuable messages, such as "We care for each other", and also other messages that I needed to re-examine, such as "We Quakers have a better way of doing things than most people" or "Such and such a type of person is not like us". I also learned not to expect much affirmation in Quaker circles. The affirmation of the handshake all round at the end of Meeting has become a visible demonstration of the way we value each other, but for many of us, the prevailing silence is not an affirming experience. Finding what sort of person we are, what is our gift, our office in Fox's sense, coming home to a faith community which suits us, builds both our confidence and our sense of self, and so we don't have to boost ourselves by stressing how superior we are. The confident Quaker voice comes from confident Quaker hearts.

Considerable research has been done on the relation between the type of person we are and the inner life which is natural to that type. This isn't to say other ways are better or worse, just that one way is right for me, another way is right for you. These studies have also shown that different types of people naturally prefer different images of Jesus – for some, he is the mystic visionary of John's Gospel, for others the thoughtful, open healer of Luke's account and so on. We know that different people link themselves with different friends and followers of Jesus throughout the centuries; some find the Carmelite tradition suits them, others the Methodist tradition, others the Quaker tradition. Perhaps in the future, we may be able to accept each other more easily and see the different traditions of each denomination as different authentic paths within the one broad road of faith; "for this is the true ground of love and unity, not that such a man walks and does just as I do, but because I feel the same Spirit and life in him, and that he walks in his rank, in his own order, in his proper way . . . ; and this is far more pleasing to me than if he walked just in that track wherein I walk" (Penington, *QF&P* 27.13). Again Penington emphasises integrity to one's own nature, and mutual acceptance of variety.

We have to be grounded and confident, and above all, centred, to deal with those who find such variety difficult. William Penn said you could "delight to step home within yourselves" (Penn, 1726). Thomas Kelly spoke of "an inner, secret turning to God" (*QF&P* 2.22); Brother Lawrence practised the presence of God; others speak in non-religious terms of living from one's own centre. When others tell us what we should think, or what we should feel, or that they are right and we are wrong, we can be firm and rooted in our own truth.

I sometimes find it helpful, particularly in Meeting, to try to put myself in another person's place, physically and mentally: "If I were sitting where she is sitting, I would see the sycamore tree through the windows, and I would see more of the other people in the Meeting – she's sitting rather isolated, I wonder if she doesn't much want to be with other people just now? Or maybe it just happened that way?"

Occasionally it's good to use a method of inner discipline diametrically different from your type, as a change, and a refreshment of the undeveloped parts of you. So the intellectual, abstract and verbally-sophisticated Quaker is revitalised by playing with clay, by gardening, by creating the Quaker Tapestry, by singing with the Leaveners, by using Celtic types of worship, and so on. The starved parts of our personal pattern of creation are fed. In MBTI terms, the Franciscan tradition is the type most different from normal Quaker practice, so we may find this a valuable way, with its practical, literally hands-on simple actions and phrases and Francis' emphasis on the value of creation. It's a very earthy spirituality, full of "humus", earth in its most basic form, and perhaps this down-to-earthness, this humility can help us with our failings of fantasising and pride. Like the whole idea of personality "types", these are of course generalisations: every individual and every tradition has its subtleties, its varieties and its contradictions. Nevertheless, such categorisation has value in highlighting what may be strongest in our selves or our group, and what may be in need of nurture.

We have a distinct Quaker tradition of inner growth and development. Rex Ambler's rediscovery of the seventeenth century Light Meditation is perhaps the most comprehensive British study, described in his *Truth of the Heart* and *A Light to Live By*. Among American Friends, Patricia Loring and Bill and Fran Taber have also recently put the Quaker tradition down on paper (Loring, 1997; Bill Taber, 1992; Fran Taber, 1997).

As our outreach grows, it will be useful to set down some of our discoveries, to expand in understandable language our own technical terms like "centring down", "holding in the Light", "discernment" and so on, and also to re-discover the experience behind some of the eighteenth century Friends' language about worship and ministry as "breathing towards God" and "speaking to states".

Confidence without dogmatism

Confidence brings problems. We can learn to be clear and definite without being dogmatic; this is vital as we talk with newcomers and with young people and children in the Quaker movement. We are making Quaker thinking and living a visible and practical option for them, offering a type of discipleship which we hope may help. Young people, children and seekers ask one big question of us: do these people really believe, and do they live by what they believe, or are they all hypocrites, perhaps unintentionally? So our confidence has to have integrity, and to be plainly rooted in our lives as well as in our thinking.

When we lack confidence in our own way of being, we are especially worried by others who are different from us and who express themselves strongly and with confidence. A recent study by Susan Robson of conflict in Quaker meetings (Robson, 2005) has shown some of the reasons for this, and suggests some of the strategies we can use to resolve it; she suggests that we can use stories in particular to help us here. Most stories describe the elaboration of tension, and develop a dynamic narrative pattern over a period of time during which the tension reaches a crisis and is then resolved. Tension is implicit in time. Telling stories is a method we use a lot in our teaching and learning, but we don't see it so much in our ministry, which usually has the form of a lyric poem or a simple statement. Often this form of ministry conveys a sense of eternal truths, but it can hide the tension and conflict of reaching those truths. Tension makes us uncomfortable and we don't demonstrate it or put ourselves through it willingly. When other Quakers impose tension on us, we object. It's as if, when we enter the Society, we imagine an unspoken promise: "The Quaker peace testimony means that no-one will ever make you upset or uncomfortable in the slightest way" and if this unformulated contract seems to be broken, we feel angry, we say "This isn't what it says on the tin!" and we mourn the loss of the golden age, the perfect clockwork Quaker group, maybe one in which everyone thinks exactly like us.

If in fact we are in a story and not in a lyric poem, if we are creating our meeting's story together as we go along, not making a perfect Quaker meeting frozen in permafrost, then tension, difference, discussion, forgiveness and reconciliation are vital, life-giving. We show our Quakerism not by denying tension and difference but by how we work with them, handle them and think about them. Might our shared silence be the sieve through which we pass the earthy compost of our disagreements? Sometimes it's good just to sit quietly and to see what issues are really big enough to worry about, and what we can just let fall through to nourish our shared and colourful garden. Sometimes forgiven hearts melt, and the springs flow.

What we've considered has been a matter of style and method rather than content – the way Quakers do practical theology, rather than the conclusions we come to. There is an important content to our thinking, but the way we arrive at that content is just as important, and is equally part of our message. When we have a gathering for people who are asking about Quakerism, we often have a panel of three speakers, giving a variety of views rather than one single authoritative voice; this style, the way the three work together, demonstrates how we think as much as their words describe what we think. In the 2006 Swarthmore Lecture, *Reflections from a Long Marriage* (Sawtell and Sawtell, 2006), two people with decades of experience of an intentional community reflected on the practical theology of living in community. Meetings can learn from their conclusions. Our commitment to respect for each other's search and each other's findings is consistent with our concept of God as multi-faceted, knowable in a group, so that my understanding of God is incomplete without yours. Can we build our worshipping communities confidently, valuing our differences, accepting our varied and different stories and experiences, learning from each other? Some of our tensions spring from our limitations, our finitude and our situation in time; in the eternity of meeting for worship, can we live with each other without urgently pushing for a release of the tension which gives us some of our spring, our drive for action?

Jill Slee Blackadder's poem "The Rainbow", published in *Quakerism, a way of life* (1982), has been a central part of my mental furniture since I first read it:

> Red said to Blue
> "My Friend how can this be
> you do not pray as joyfully as me?"

> Blue said, replying
> "Red, you tell me why
> you never pray as soulfully as I?"

> To Green said Yellow
> "Why is it my Friend,
> that when you pray you never kneel or bend?"

Green said to Yellow
"Do you call that pray?
I disagree, that's not the proper way."

Then up came Indigo and Orange too
with different ways of praying,
old and new.

Poor Violet went quite pale,
as if afraid.
It was to all a secret how she prayed.

"Oh, colours," then said God.
"Each one of you is mine.
For how, without my light,
could you so shine.

Pray as your colour bids you
Never cease to glow.
I need your differences
They make my bow."

8. Spiritual Compost

Knowing the bad stuff

Compost is popular these days! Our local council is busy promoting recycling, and it's a good metaphor for how we deal with the bad stuff: making it into something good, turning the negative into the positive, accepting the messiness, leaving time for the breakdown and re-creation, living in harmony with a natural process. However, the poetic analogy needs unpacking – and as always when we work with rotten stuff, we need a strong stomach. Some of it is unpleasant.

In our faithfulness and in our discipleship, we "deal with the bad stuff" – the negative aspects of ourselves and of the world, the violence, the cruelty, the terrible tragedies, the senseless destruction in the natural world – in three senses and from three points of view: we experience it ourselves, as bad things happen to us and we do bad things; we work with it in ourselves and in others, to stop it and set it right; and we try to fit it into our philosophical and theological worldview, with integrity.

All these approaches to the bad stuff illuminate each other. Some of us know tragedy, inner splitting and turmoil, in the core of our selves; terrible and wrong things have been done to us or have happened to us, or we have ourselves done wrong; we know misery and evil in our guts and our hearts. Some of us, as peace workers, teachers, prison ministers, police officers, nurses and doctors, social workers, civil servants, work hands-on with the perversity of humankind and of nature, and have a practical understanding which can both illuminate and earth the theoretical arguments of those who think and reflect. And in different degrees, each of us does all of them: we all act, reflect and act again, we take our quiet worship into the world and we take the world into our silence.

Here we are exploring more deeply one of our original questions, "God, who am I?", and we find that the question is broader: "Who are we, who can do these awful things to each other?" Technically, we are looking at our understanding of humanity, society, sin and evil.

John Woolman's experience (*QF&P* 21.64) when he was ill with pleurisy can help us to grasp this. He saw "a mass of human beings in as great misery as they could be, and live, and I was mixed in with them, and henceforth might not consider myself as a distinct or separate being." Illness and suffering help us to see ourselves as part of ordinary humanity, "in the mixture"; we have learnt this too from our work in the ecological movement, that we are all involved in damage to creation, and in repairing it. The truthful answer to "God, who am I?" is often "You are part of the planet's problem", or "You are not as skilful as you think you are", or "You have hurt your friend". We can bring the truth about ourselves into the Light in our quiet worship, and recognise and accept our own failings and humanness.

The bad stuff which I have worked with most is the sexual abuse of children, a huge and difficult issue with which I struggled, as we all have as a Society. To reply to the question, "What experience lies behind these words?", I have not myself suffered abuse; the issue came into the Society's public consciousness during my time as General Secretary of Quaker Home Service; my experience is of working with many Quaker responses to it.

People who have endured abuse as children find it stressful to talk about; bringing the experience into the Light oneself is difficult, let alone asking others to keep it in the Light. So secrecy feels simpler. The most dreadful result of abuse is the twisting and destruction of the personality, the terrible wounding of self-respect, the armouring of the heart against any future hurt, the defensive padding which might give some protection. Many turn to drugs or alcohol, or endure long-term mental illness; for some, suicide is a way out. Healing might be possible but a huge scar remains. A loving, respectful and accepting community is needed, within which people can name terror and misery even if only inwardly, behind the merciful veil of silence; skilled professionals can help, but alongside that, survivors need an ordinary friendly group, within which love can grow again in an atmosphere of healing and re-creation – a whole community in which all have the opportunity to give help and love to each other.

After the brutal violation, in the dark womb of the mind a strange fertilisation can take place and a new creation might germinate, an understanding of inner anguish, a cry for justice against the power or authority which has done this wrong, or a determination to found a centre for healing.

This is not just girls' experience. Boys are abused; some Quaker men are bringing their invisible trauma into the light, and in our Society which transcends gender, men too can conceive inwardly the loving fruit of loveless violation and turn it to good. Those who have been abusers, and who may have been abused themselves in the past, also need a community in which to heal and grow, and learn love.

In our community's task of nursing, healing and prevention, respect is crucial. Our principle of looking for that of God in everyone teaches us to treat children with a sense of their own core value; they are not treated as pawns in power games; they are respected. This approach can give them inward strength, so that the hooks of abusive power have nothing to latch on to.

How does this issue relate to our task of reflecting on the bad stuff?

Learning outside the walls

When John Woolman realised that he was mixed in with suffering humanity, he also realised the limitations of his own Quaker Society's image of itself as a self-sufficient group, an enclosed garden, not like other people. We still keep elements of this image in our picture of the Quaker group, where we consider we have sorted out the problems and live rightly. As we worked with the issue of abuse, I sometimes heard Friends say, "Do we have to bring in the social workers and the police – can't we just deal with this case which has come up, in our own group, and keep it in the family?" Keeping things in the family is the problem! The walls of the garden must be taken down; Paradise contains the snake. Integrity requires us to be courageous, honest and truthful as we consider and reflect on our own community and wider society.

In poetic, mythological and symbolic language the move out from Paradise is the story of the development away from that first perfect way of life, when everything lived "answerable to the design of our creation". The original narrative in Genesis does not use the word "Fall", which is a later interpretation. We cannot separate out creation and development; they are simultaneous, because the very fact that God has (using the symbolic language) created us separate from God, with freedom to choose, implies at least the possibility and all too often the real fact that we will choose to move away from the Divine, and to hide.

We could retreat here to a pious exhortation, "Go back to God, stick close to the Divine." Yes, but that does not mean retreating from exposure to reality. To use an everyday example, I think back to the day our son passed his driving test, and we handed the car keys over to him and said, "Off you go! Have a wonderful time!" When we are growing up, we probably don't consider the significance of getting the car keys – we are more focused on what we are going to do! – but any parent with imagination thinks of the dangers as well as the wonderful possibilities. Yet we have to let the children go. For most of us that day of independence and freedom is inevitable from the day our child was born. The car metaphor is just a vivid example. Others could be the first steps, the first day at school, the first holiday away from the family. Separations, choices for which we have prepared our children. Can our concept of God include God's enjoyment of our independence? Is this development, with its potential for error and tragedy, a necessary part of creation?

At the back of this imagery is Dietrich Bonhoeffer's resonant phrase "Man come of Age". In letters written on 8th and 16th July 1944, he says:

> . . . I am so anxious that God should not be relegated to some last secret place, but that we should frankly recognise that the world and men have come of age, that we should not speak ill of man in his worldliness, but confront him with God at his strongest point. . . . There is no longer any need for God as a working hypothesis, whether in morals, politics or science. Nor is there any need for such a God in religion or philosophy. In the name of intellectual honesty these working hypotheses should be dropped.
> (Bonhoeffer, 1981, pp.160 and 163)

We know something of the experience which lies behind these words. Bonhoeffer did not write this in the security of a middle-class suburb in peacetime; in July 1944 he was in the military section of Tegel prison, woken every night at 1.30am by British air raids, and fairly clear that he would be executed at some point. He knew the results of human independence. Quakers who are non-theists have taken this thinking further, dropping the hypothesis of God in the gaps of our knowledge in favour of a much more diffused understanding of the

Divine; they are – to use David Boulton's phrase – "Godless for God's sake".

I find I need some images, as long as I know they are images, and I value the word-picture from a Friend who replied to the survey I referred to in the last chapter:

> I used to drive to work each morning and would stop in a line of traffic where the road forked. I would be overtaken by a group of three, a mother and two smallish children on bicycles. They were all kitted out for maximum visibility and safety, and would go cautiously and rather wobblyly as a threesome across the line of oncoming traffic. When they reached the new road, the mother would draw to one side and without a backward look the two children would seriously wobble onwards, as she watched them into the distance. There was nothing else she could do now but let them learn. That seemed to me to encapsulate something about the nature of God. That's how it works for me.

The underlying metaphors here are all images of going out beyond the safety of the primeval garden and the home, images of growing away and up, of travelling, wobbling, learning, falling and hurting ourselves and others. "Kitted out for maximum safety" is one clue for us in a world where abuse takes place, where tsunamis destroy communities and ecosystems, and where some of the social problems are so endemic that decades of work are needed. As well as working for safety, we need to think about and work with risks. One Friend who works in the prison service wrote of her perception that Quakers tended to avoid facing the reality of evils. Referring to some pagan and indigenous Ways which sought to do no harm but to protect, she said that her practice was to intervene practically or spiritually, even at the possible cost of temporarily increasing the chaos.

Can we, in the Buddhist term, be "skilful" in our independent freedom? We need to know what we are doing. Out in the world, as people who have come of age in our thinking about God and other human beings, can we find and embrace an innocence which is not blind and thoughtless?

We can reflect at depth, faithfully and with courage about God's sharing in creation. Like the mother waiting behind as her children cycle away, God lets us do dangerous things, taking risks with us, going into the core of human darkness and wrong, entrusting us to each others' care. If the Divine, the creative origin of our story and our being, enters creatively into the tension of the story with us, and shares in its creation along with all of us, what becomes possible? Can the anguish be healed, can we resolve some of the conflicts and difficulties?

What if our own answer to the question "God, who am I?" is, "I am a person who has done something clearly wrong – I am sinful, I am guilty"?

It's hard to live with the knowledge of the wrong things we have done, hard to accept that we need forgiveness. In the Society of Friends we have no ways I know of for handling this in a religious way; we tend to fall back on hand-me-downs from pop psychology. We might reflect on three stories.

Once when I explained that Quakers think of all life as potentially sacramental, a young woman responded brightly, "Every meal can be a communion, yes – so is every bath a baptism?" That's an extension of Quaker thinking that we have never picked up, but it's logical. We wash ourselves to be fit to start a new day, to live with other people, to free ourselves from old grime, to safeguard our physical health . . .

Yukitaka Yamamoto was a Japanese naval "political officer" in New Guinea in the 1939–45 war. On his return, he decided to carry out the Shinto water purification, *misogi*, at the Tsubaki Grand Shrine, both to free himself from the terrible memories and to prepare himself to take up a ministry of peacemaking. *Misogi* entails various ritual actions and prayers, followed by standing for several minutes under a natural waterfall in the beautiful grounds of the Shrine; in winter the temperature is well below freezing. Yamamoto performed *misogi* every single day for ten years (Yamamoto, 1999).

Finally, a Friend once talked with me concerning a sense of guilt about something in his past. I remembered my own experience of confession, when as a representative of God, a priest declared that I was absolved and my guilt taken away, and sent me away with the traditional words "Go in peace; and pray for me too, a sinner". I concluded that my friend needed to hear a similar clear declaration that he was forgiven, and with as much authority as I could muster,

I said that God had forgiven both of us where we had fallen short.
I don't know what effect that had – one doesn't in these circumstances.

We need to think more deeply about how people work with guilt. The purpose of forgiveness and reconciliation is that we are included in the community; perhaps the Quaker signal of this is our handshake after Meeting. Or the invitation to join the washing-up after coffee, another watery experience. But do these friendly Friends know the guilts which, rationally or irrationally, we may carry? How do we help each other come outside our protective yet isolating walls? Maybe composting our lives starts with accepting our own messiness, letting it take its time to enrich us, and make us stronger and more confident, more grounded. Neither water nor words can take away the past. But they can perhaps help us work with it, breaking it down, releasing its nutrients. Compost actually makes new ground, new fertile foundations – can new life spring up within us from the rubbish of our mistakes?

9. Quakers, Cross and Resurrection

Quakers and the cross

How do we understand the cluster of images and metaphors which gather round the crucifixion and resurrection of Jesus? This part of the anthology of tradition is significant for Friends in other yearly meetings, and it has been helpful for British Friends in the past. Has the story anything to offer us as we reflect on the problems of suffering and wrongdoing, and the hope of newness?

Today, British Friends find any discussion of "the cross" difficult, as do many liberal Christians. We are deeply uncomfortable with the inadequate or repellent pictures of God and of human beings which apparently lie behind the words when people say things like, "Jesus died to reconcile us to God by his blood, and to set us free from our sins by his sacrifice in our place." We do not want to look for a deeper meaning; we doubt if it is worth the effort. The imagery of being freed by blood is repulsive; the answers seem to come too easily. For many of us, the whole bundle of thinking about Jesus' death is an unnecessary burden we gladly left behind when we abandoned the elementary lessons of our past, and came to Quakers.

But it's worth looking at some of the ideas about Jesus' death and its effects for us, because we often reject them without examining our reasons. Often the metaphors in which the ideas are expressed simply don't speak to us. But beyond the metaphors is the idea, and beyond that, the experience. Let's ask our quakerly question and see where that leads us. "What experience lies behind these words?"

The experience of many people through two thousand years has been that when they have contemplated the death of Jesus, they have felt some sense of unlocking and relief; a release of tension; re-creation; liberation. I can only speak of my own experience here, and then seek to move from that to empathise with the feelings of others. I step cautiously because at depth I have never felt totally alienated, and so I don't have the real sense of reconnection and re-making which for some is the core of the experience. I have felt this only once, at a performance of *Godspell*, a 1970s presentation of the life of Jesus shown through clowning and song. After two hours of abundant life, in which we were all thoroughly caught up and involved, the actor playing Jesus was spread on the wire fence at the back of the stage and sang, "O God, I'm bleeding, O God, I'm dying, O God, I'm dead", and we sat held together in silence. I felt grief and horror and the release of tension; I thought, "That's what all the words mean", and that for me has been a reference point ever since.

The first Quakers spoke of "the Cross" of bearing witness to their convictions. Mary Penington tells us, "I was exercised against [i.e. I thought very hard about] taking up the Cross to the language, fashions, customs, titles, honour, and esteem in the world; my relations made this Cross very heavy" (QF&P 19.13, preamble). Friends were convinced that "Christ has come to teach his people himself". The foundation of their faith was their direct experience of God: they carried this into every aspect of their lives with such integrity that they refused to swear oaths in court or to pay tithes to the established church to support the paid clergy; they similarly refused, in the hierarchical society of their day, to take off their hats to anyone, to give people honorific titles or to wear the frills and furbelows of rank. Like James Nayler, many Friends paid the price in prison sentences, physical suffering, contempt, fines and ridicule.

Luke Cock's description of his experience of the Weeping Cross, quoted above (p. 57) shows the same experience as that of Mary Penington, though at the other end of the social scale. Quaker children, going through the streets in their distinctive clothes, were stoned (QF&P 19.42). In 1664, Priscilla Cotton said:

> Friends, the Cross is the power of God. When you flee the Cross, you lose the power . . . As you wait in the Light, you will come to know a Cross in the use of meat, drink and apparel; and keep to the Cross when alone or in company; what the pure mind of God stands against in you, that the Cross is against.
>
> (*Piety Promoted*, 1706, p.10)

Friends chose these ways of making visible the tension between the values of the contemporary world we inhabit, in time, and the values of the eternal world in which we also live.

As the Society developed, the tension was made more bearable by retreating into the "enclosed garden" of the Quaker community within which the plain language and clothes were normal. In Britain Yearly Meeting today we still see the effects of this image of our Quaker society as a distinct walled-off group, within which we can indulge ourselves and be like little children; we often make it difficult for others to get in. Thankfully, today we are very much more "mixed in" with the world. But what sense do we still have of the tension between the values of this present time and the values of the eternal world?

God in all life

Friends have said that Jesus died because of the way he lived in tension with the values of his world. Is there anything more? We can certainly learn from all this today, and be strengthened to witness to our values; but the cross is not just about a tension of values, or putting up with ridicule, or working out a discipline for our daily lives. The whole Christian understanding of it is far bigger than this.

Jesus was crucified on the local rubbish-tip. "The cross" expresses the Spirit of God entering into the most foul and disgusting ways we can go wrong, the most rotten ways we can live and do things to each other; the cross says that the Spirit is fully here, taking part, enduring, with us. If our spirituality is truly grounded in the total suffusing of all life with the Spirit, God is here too, suffering and dying.

If we are made unhappy by considering the experience of suffering, we often react by trying to deny its validity as a real present experience for those who are going through pain and anguish. I have sometimes heard Friends imply that "if you become a Quaker, you won't suffer. And if all the world were Quaker, there wouldn't be suffering." This is so patently exaggerated that we don't actually put it into these words but such an attitude underlies some of our words. Because we can't alleviate it and it makes us uncomfortable, I have sometimes heard us try to deny the bitter experience of racism, of homophobia, of childlessness, of grief.

We respond to suffering in deeply negative ways, kicking the cat, passing on the anguish, hurting ourselves and others individually and globally; but it will be more productive for us to consider the creative responses of which we are capable. I have to speak here with humility and caution, since I have not gone through many times of anguish and loss. I have experienced two periods of depression, definitely an experience of negativity, but not for me a time of pain.

Faced with the bitter experience of physical and mental suffering, people have taken it into their deepest hearts and have tried to make sense of it by all creative means – in music and art of all types, in humour, in poetry, philosophy, prayer, worship. We want the bad experience to stop, naturally, but also we need it to be affirmed and validated, not just wiped out. It is part of us, part of the tension of our story, part of being Black in Britain, part of the life of the gay community, and it is the raw material from which we create blues singing, the community of grief, endless charitable work, and the radical transforming energy of those who come out from the shadows of stigmatisation. In the spirituality of some denominations, suffering and brokenness are lifted up in the communion service, and become life-giving. Where do Friends proclaim this reality?

I find that what I ask for is actually help in carrying my own small cross, or rather the variety of tiny crosses in my life; my own nature with its difficulties, little things that have happened, bad things I have done. I don't particularly want the whole lot taken away, it's part of my life; I just want it acknowledged, and I want to feel that perhaps I can give my little cross to be taken up into the cosmic sharing of the pain of the world.

Maybe, since we are a varied group of people, we might want to consider the cross and the resurrection through a variety of approaches, each rooted in the nature of our varied and different creations, and ask ourselves, at least in our inner silence, if this powerful story speaks to us in any way. Beginning with Jesus himself, people have used Jesus' crucifixion and resurrection as a way of holding together their understanding of God and their understanding of the anguish of the world. As we deal with pain, wrongdoing and suffering, on the practical and the philosophical levels, we must take them into account in our thinking about God and then, like John Woolman, we will want to go out to alleviate and heal the anguish, distress, cruelty, injustice and wrong in the world which we are mixed into. It may be helpful to see if there is any truth underlying the images and concepts which we have discarded; at the least, looking at how they developed can help us see how our own thinking may develop in the future. We may as a result have more inner resources to help us work to put things right.

Part of our own Quaker problem is that modern Friends have rightly rejected a simplistic statement of the significance of the cross, unhappy with the violence of the image as well as the meanings given to it. And beyond that is a hidden problem in the Quaker world today and in our recent history. Many Quakers in other parts of the world, and almost all British Quakers of the nineteenth century, use language about the cross and about Jesus' death and resurrection which we today call evangelical. Books by Quaker writers such as the American Richard Foster today, and the British Hannah Whittall-Smith from the nineteenth century, sell well in bookshops in the UK which hesitate to stock *Quaker Faith & Practice*. We are not reconciled with our own evangelical Quaker past, and many of us find our worldwide Quaker present difficult to cope with. I suspect, however, that some British Quakers like linking up with other churches and with the worldwide family of Friends just because that gives us licence to take part in forms of worship and to explore thinking which we could not possibly articulate in our own meetings. As we continue in ecumenical dialogue, and as Quakers work together on a world scale, we have to learn to understand each other's words about Jesus' death and resurrection.

Evangelical Christians are so called because for them the Gospel is "Good News" – *God-speill* in Anglo-Saxon, *evangelion*, meaning "the Good Message" in Greek. So they have made the Gospel message as easy to understand, as unsophisticated and simple as possible, and taught it as early as possible as a statement, a solid foundation for life and belief. Some British Quakers find evangelical language helpful, and the Christian Quaker Renewal Group is a lively and growing part of the British Quaker scene today. Many Friends are glad to speak of the close relationship they have with the Spirit of Jesus in their hearts, and as a daily presence in their lives.

One reason I am evangelical about Quakerism – part of its Good News for me – is that we emphasise that human thinking develops and changes, and that the inner experience is more important than the words which express it. The words we dislike in many evangelical Christians express their experience; as adults, they have thought them through and choose to go on or to begin using them. For many Quakers, we know that what we learnt as children has to be evaluated, re-thought, and then laid aside or accepted as metaphor.

The eloquence of the arts

We can explore some of these ideas through the visual arts. Faced with the horror of human sickness and pain, and of our cruel treatment of each other, many people have looked at the death of Jesus on the cross and created works of art to express their reflections on it.

I recently saw a crucifix made by a British squaddie serving in Belfast. He made the cross from the barbed wire of the Peace Line. Jesus is hanging on the wire cross; his disfigured face and slender body are made from the fawn standard-issue toilet paper given to each soldier; his hands, at the end of toilet-paper arms, are formed by the barbs of the wire; his hair and loincloth came from one of the army's dark brown sandbags. This crucifix is a reflection on Jesus' suffering and death, made in materials which were part of its creator's daily life.

The terrible Isenheim Altarpiece, painted in about 1515 by Mathis Grunewald, means more if we understand where it came from. It was painted for a hospital for people with erysipelas, a severe inflammation of the skin. Jesus is shown dying in anguish, his skin covered in sores. The hospital patients had, as their focus for prayer, the man whom they thought of as the Son of God, suffering exactly as they were.

This Altarpiece was deliberately echoed by Otto Dix, a German artist. He was Professor of Art at the Academy in Dresden when he painted his War Triptych in 1932, showing soldiers going into battle, the aftermath of gunfire and shelling, with the legs and barbed-wire-crowned head of Grunewald's Christ among the rubble, and the grim rescue of one wounded man from a pile of the dead. The truth of this picture was so painful, even 14 years after a war which many wanted forgotten, that Dix was sacked and banned from exhibiting his work (MacGregor, 2000).

These, and many other depictions of Jesus on the cross in art or music, incorporate the experience of both artist and beholder. Contemplating these various images of crucifixion enlarges my understanding of the feelings of people wrenched by inescapable sickness and war.

Silent contemplation is one way into these mysteries, and many of us prefer it. However, because we are people who talk, we have attempted for some two thousand years to put into the words and thought-forms of our own particular time a rational description of the effects of Jesus' death. Let's look at some of these understandings, explore the experience behind them and the imagery in which they are expressed, and see whether they speak to us today. None of them is meant to be a total, final statement of the meaning of Jesus' death, and we can cheerfully let them go if they don't speak to our condition, or if we feel that the concept of God which underlies them is so inadequate as to be unhelpful.

The medieval poem *The Dream of the Rood* shows us one picture of the death of Jesus which appealed strongly to its hearers. The Cross itself tells the story:

> Then I saw the King of all mankind
> In brave mood hasting to mount upon me.
> Refuse I dared not, nor bow or break.
> . . .
> Then the young Warrior, God the All-Wielder,
> Put off his raiment, steadfast and strong;
> With lordly mood in the sight of many
> He mounted the Cross to redeem mankind.
> When the Hero clasped me I trembled in terror,
> But I dared not bow me nor bend to earth;
> I must needs stand fast. Upraised as the Rood
> I held the High King, the Lord of Heaven.
>
> (Kennedy, 1963)

In the early middle ages, the king of any nation had to lead his soldiers into battle, and endure considerable physical suffering. In the terms and thought-forms of this period, Jesus was seen as "Christ the Victor". The author of the *Dream* emphasises also Jesus' initiative, so all the verbs are active: "he put off his raiment . . . he mounted the Cross." Ten centuries later, many of us pick out in the Gospel stories the elements which show Jesus' submission to and endurance of what was done to him, such as his clothes being taken from him, his patient suffering. The *Dream* shows us a different world from the quiet suburban meeting house – though maybe we can recognise the experience of the inner city. Its imagery is of warriors and victories – and some churches today sing wonderful Easter hymns about armies with banners, fights and glorious battles: not Friends' natural language.

But on one occasion this poem, which I have loved for years, gave me a great deal of strength; in Friends House we were cutting our budgets and making a lot of redundancies and as a manager, I had to put these cuts into effect and tell some staff that they would be made redundant. Like the Rood in the poem, I was the instrument of execution; I trembled in terror, but I must needs stand fast.

Another model became popular a few centuries later, when European society had developed from warrior kings leading warring tribes, to the chivalrous feudal system in which lesser human beings owed allegiance and honour to their overlord; a squire owed work and honour to his feudal lord, who in turn owed it to the king. If anyone committed an offence against his overlord, he either received the due punishment or gave "satisfaction" in the form of money, which restored the overlord's honour.

Anselm (1033–1109), in his book *Cur Deus Homo?* (*Why did God become Man?*), developed his understanding of the effects of Jesus' death in these terms. In his imagery, Man has dishonoured God, his overlord, by his wrongdoing; Man is unable to provide the necessary satisfaction, but God has provided a means of satisfaction by sending his Son, who assumed humanity and, as a man, received the due punishment by dying innocently; so he restored God's honour. This "satisfaction theory" was widely and rapidly accepted, because it used the systems and thought-forms of Anselm's own times. Today it is almost impossible for us to understand; it would be interesting to know if this model is useful in other social systems, where "honour" and "face" are significant.

If we move forward another few centuries, a less immediately personal, more centralised system of law had taken hold. God was imagined through this new way of thought; he was seen as perfectly just, and his law as inviolable. God's justice was an unquestioned given; this justice demanded punishment on a heavenly scale, in exactly the same way as justice led to punishment in people's everyday lives. This logic was seen by all to be fair, and a necessary protection against chronic social and political unrest. So the theologians of the Reformation worked out the penal theory of the way Jesus' death was effective. Because of the importance of the rule of law and the sense that things had gone wrong in human lives, someone had to be punished; Jesus bore the punishment instead of us, and thus enabled God to forgive sin and to remain perfect in his justice.

By this time many Friends will be totally repelled by all these theological notions and utterly confirmed in our traditional distaste for concepts of God and man which we have rejected long ago. We can rightly reject or lay aside the outward forms of Christian teaching which were expressed in terms of the historical social and philosophical ideas of past centuries, but we then have to ask ourselves: what aspects of today's thought-forms and social settings are we unthinkingly and unreflectively using in our own models about God and about ourselves? Or our own lack of models?

A fourth model or description of the way in which the death of Jesus can work in our hearts and minds has been called the moral theory. Peter Abelard (1079–1142) put this most clearly when he taught that the picture of God's suffering love, of Jesus crucified by the selfishness, pride and wrongness of human beings, makes a strong appeal to us: by contemplating so grievous an image, we are inwardly reconciled and changed. In our own Quaker tradition, John Wilhelm Rowntree expresses this in one of the few extended discussions of the Cross included in *Faith & Practice*: "See in the crucifixion . . . the flashing into light of an eternal fact, the pain we inflict on his heart by our own wrongdoing . . . God shows you his sufferings" (*QF&P* 26.49). Notice that both Rowntree and Abelard use words about looking – "See in the crucifixion . . . "; "the picture of God's suffering love" – these are words about contemplation and visual imagery. In *Seeing Salvation*, Neil MacGregor linked the mediaeval development of this model to the contemporary development of painting and the visual arts. In the historic development of the Christian tradition, it is also linked to Francis of Assisi's visual presentation of the birth and death of Jesus. In 1223 in Greccio, he was the first to show the nativity scene to the people, an actual crib in a real stable, with real animals; and he and his friars showed the reality of humility and poverty both visually and practically by their imitation of Jesus' way of life. In our Quaker way of worship some of us find inner visual imagery useful; we have learned to appreciate film and theatre as a method of presenting truth, and have rediscovered the visual arts. We also encourage each other to "let our lives speak".

The concept of God which underlies this model is less unattractive than some of the earlier concepts we have described – God become human only has the power of love and the power of suffering, simply making a mute appeal to us as we look. However, this risks leaving out altogether any understanding of God's toughness, strength and power, and the themes of conquest over sin and of victory.

Human beings have experienced some sort of release from whatever in their past has bound and restricted them; they have linked this release with the death of Jesus and have interpreted the experience in the thought-forms of their own day. Understanding this can liberate us to feel for the place where their words about the death of Jesus have come from, to try to enter imaginatively into their world-view, and to reflect on the truth behind and around all these words.

What are our modern images, what in our own experience can we use to express the deep sense of the effect of Jesus' death and resurrection for us? Can we enter into this experience in any way and, as part of our "travelling documents", can we produce our own models, accepting their limitations even before we start? Do we have anything to say here to the rest of the Christian tradition? We must make sure that the concept of God which underlies our model is big enough, and that we take into account the range and depth of the world's suffering and anguish.

Jesus' meaning

What significance did Jesus give to his own death? Is it possible to find the way back to what he said about it, and to ask our question, "What experience lies behind these words?" He certainly expected death of some sort, though he may well have expected the Jewish punishment of stoning rather than the Roman one of crucifixion. It's worth noting that often when he spoke of his own death before it took place, Jesus apparently didn't talk about any meaning it might have, just that it was inevitable: "the Son of Man must suffer". But according to the Gospel records he used three images to point towards the meaning of his own death and continuing life: the germinating seed, childbirth, and eating meals together. All three pick up our theme of creation and re-creation; they point forwards rather than backwards, to renewal rather than to annihilation.

When Greek enquirers came saying "we want to see Jesus", he

talked with them in the metaphors and language of the Greek nature and mystery religions. "Truly I tell you, unless a grain of wheat falls into the ground and dies, it remains alone. But if it dies it bears much fruit" (John 12:20–25). The living seed, to take part in the cycle of creation, must change, lose its nature and explode with the power of its inner life – if it holds on to its body, its outer husk of structure, its potential is lost.

"When a woman is in labour, she has pain, because her hour has come; but when her child is born, she no longer remembers the anguish because of the joy of having brought a human being into the world" (John 16:21). The cycle of creation and the hard work of bringing forth life from within lie behind this image too. Jesus didn't deny the experience of suffering in childbirth even though he didn't experience it himself; he talked of it as ultimately creative.

Just before his death Jesus gave his friends an interpretation of their usual meals together which would help them to reflect on his death after he was gone (Luke 22:19–20). The Jesus Community continued to eat and drink together and developed a variety of ways of doing this, ways and practices which are still developing and changing as people go on finding new meanings in them. Many people in the churches over many centuries have found that sharing in the communion service helps them to reflect on Jesus' death and resurrection and to understand it more deeply. If our thinking is based on experience, we cannot deny this accumulated experience; it's worth trying to understand it more deeply, even if we choose not to go down this path. There is no one correct way of understanding this meal, any more than there is only one correct way of producing *Hamlet* – we can go on reinterpreting it and understanding more and more about it. I value the communion service because in it we take brokenness into worship, we hold it up, we affirm that it can be life-giving and we share it. But each person who shares this meal understands it slightly differently; and the Spirit can be in all of them. The Quaker element in this tradition is our affirmation that every meal can be a way to witness to transforming and creative life.

These three images are ways in which Jesus saw meaning in his own suffering and death. He did not want it, for he loved life, and his unanswered prayer was that he should go on living. But like the early Friends, he lived by the inner principles of God's truth and the clash was unavoidable. He certainly knew what to expect; when he was about ten, the Romans crushed a rebellion in Galilee and Judaea, and 3,000 Jews were crucified along all the roads of the country as a deterrent. Jesus is likely to have seen them, and this dark experience probably became part of his reflection about the way God works and acts.

When we revised *Quaker Faith & Practice* in 1994, many Quakers were concerned that Jesus' being raised from death was not mentioned very often. But as we discussed it afterwards, Jo Farrow said robustly, "You can't keep the resurrection down! It keeps popping up – that's its nature!" As Jesus' disciples experienced his continuing life with them in a new form, one common thread in the stories is that his presence wasn't obvious; he was alive, but different; they couldn't recognise him in quite the same way. The gift of new life is re-creation, not resuscitation; it is a present and a future of growth and newness, not of everlasting preservation; it is renewal and bounce, after betrayal, loss and annihilation.

To return to our image of compost, the compost heap is dark with the darkness of the Saturday after Good Friday and before Easter Day; it takes time to mature, but it is alive with potential. "There lives the dearest freshness deep down things" (Gerard Manley Hopkins, "God's Grandeur"). The negative can burst out with the springing power of new life. Jesus' friends found he was still a living and powerful force in their lives, and the presence of the Spirit of Jesus among us now is a strong element in Quaker tradition. Although we use imagery and metaphor to grasp its significance, the death and return to life of Jesus is not just a metaphor; in J.R.R. Tolkien's and C.S. Lewis's words, it is a "true myth" (Lewis, 2000, 976f), sharing in the integrity of the nature of creation itself, of God who is the stuff of creation, and of the Spirit whose ground and spring is the mercies and forgiveness of God.

10. Quaker Pathology

So sweetest things turn sourest by their deeds;
Lilies that fester smell far worse than weeds.

William Shakespeare, Sonnet 94

When we look at other Christian churches, it is easy to see their defects, and alluringly easy to dismiss their whole traditions. It may be harder to notice where things are going wrong in our Quaker life; harder still to stay with the issue when we do smell something festering and to track down the sickness to its source.

Yet we have to ask: what are the defects of our Quaker virtues? How can we stop things turning sour? And what is the right medicine, what can heal us when we have festered and gone pathologically wrong?

We hope that our silent worship and our faithfulness to the search for truth develops in us a certain clarity of vision. When we turn the light of that clarity on Britain Yearly Meeting itself, on the lives of our own meetings and on our own inner lives, some discomforting evidence shows up of good solid Quaker virtues which have become defects, attitudes which have developed for sound reasons but which have become fixed, unexamined and unhelpful.

As we look at some of these conditions, we may be helped by the thoughts and views of non-Quakers who are able to see us objectively. People who come to find out about Quakers and discover we are not right for them often have some interesting things to say; so do new Quakers in our local meetings and non-Quaker staff in Friends House. They are not fogged by preconceptions; they see things more clearly, though they are usually too courteous to put them into words, kindly shielding us from the truth.

The problems show up in three main areas – the life of our local meetings, our national life as a Society, and our own inner lives. What follows here is a series of reflections rather than any attempt at analysis – a collection of stories from my experience, which may be food for you to chew on in your own time and in your own ways.

Relating to each other in the meeting's life

"I know Quakers never thank anybody," said the long-term attender to me rather sadly, "but I have been cherishing members of this meeting for about 20 years now, and it just seems as if it is never noticed at all, or if people do notice, it's just taken for granted."

The myth that Quakers never say thank you springs from our dislike of flowery and overblown expressions of thanks, which in some communities had become routine. So not thanking became Quaker routine, and like our plain speaking, this routine can become an excuse for inconsiderate rudeness. The habit is also rooted in our conviction that service performed for the meeting, for the Society or for an individual is not done in order to earn thanks, it's done from a real sense of service and because we know that we flourish best as a community when we all share in the tasks which keep the community working. But because we don't thank people automatically or effusively, it would be sad if we lost the sense of thankfulness and the capacity to tell someone that we value what they have done.

There is an English reserve about some aspects of Quaker culture in Britain – we seem to retain the last relics of a stoical sidelining of emotion which marked a certain sort of upbringing. Is this really English, or is it also part of the culture of Friends from a Celtic background? Whatever the roots of this attitude, it is worth examining to see whether it is truly grounded in Quaker thinking, or just part of our early upbringing and our setting in history.

For many people, silence is not an affirming experience. In most circles, it is a freezing experience, a withdrawal of approval, a denial of value. Anyone in the performing arts knows the deep appreciative silence at the end of a play or a song which shows that the audience has been moved – but in this setting we have worked for a relationship between us, audience and performer together, we are alert to the currents of feeling, and silence is followed by applause. By contrast, finishing off the monthly meeting accounts is lonely hard work, and is hardly ever even noticed, still less affirmed and applauded by the Friends whose right ordering has been so faithfully served.

Really seeing other people, and seeing that of God in them, can lead us to a gracious and peaceful appreciation of all their goodness and all the small and large things they do; we can feel when it is right to put this into words or actions.

＊　＊　＊

"After the first few weeks when I was welcomed very warmly, I find that I go to Meeting and I come away again, and I wonder if anyone has noticed me at all – they are all so busy talking to each other," said someone who had been coming for several months. The rituals we may have given up from other faiths and other churches do at least embody a personal interchange which can validate the tentative individual worshipper – money is collected, the minister greets people at the door, each person is given communion or blessed.

If we truly value each person in our meeting, we will notice them. Do we actually look at each other's faces and see each other? The doorkeeper's welcoming ministry is vital to the spirit of the worship.

So many problems in the life of a meeting are prevented or overcome by good and thoughtful oversight. A group of Overseers who really notice people, who work carefully, prayerfully and faithfully together, gives the community of the meeting a solid foundation for all the fun and work, social life and study.

＊　＊　＊

When we Quakers become over-serious and over-busy, we risk a blighting barrenness of spirit. We may not drink at all, or rarely to excess, we don't over-eat; one Quaker conference I organised was criticised because the food was too good, and at another a representative muttered, "My monthly meeting doesn't pay for me to come to these events to enjoy myself."

Part of the spiritual hunger of our time is a hunger for simple friendship, for the enjoyment of life, for companions of like mind in everyday things as well as those things which are eternal. Sheffield Friends have met monthly for many years in QUAFF, Quakers United in Fun and Frivolity; meetings have parties, weekends away, walks, concerts and meals. In all of this, we create and re-create our communities and ourselves. Some of this need was met when we created the Quaker Tapestry; it was something beautiful we did together, well worth the time and effort but not deadly serious, and shared by Friends from all over the country who could create beauty, who enjoyed lovingly and carefully using their varied and different skills.

Just being friendly is part of our outreach – "Make a friend and you make a Friend", as an experienced Home Service staff member used to say. But the common thread in these three examples is valuing people as individuals for themselves and showing that we value them; and our local meetings are the places where this is tested every week. One of the unspoken questions in the heart of everyone trying out different religious groups is, "Do these people live up to what they say?"

So it's important for people coming to a meeting to be drawn into a real and appropriate friendly group – whether we meet for play-reading, children's birthdays, work together on the meeting house garden, social action, peace witness or dropping in on one another for tea, as well as all the endless committees. But we know we share a deeper basis than all these. A member of a nominations committee approached an older Friend who had recently retired, and asked her to consider serving on a local Quaker committee: "We thought that you might find it interesting to do this sort of work, now that you have more time." The Friend replied, "Quakerism is my religion, not my hobby."

*   *   *

"I am a Quaker; in case of emergency, please be silent." Yes, but . . . is silence really the only option? For many of us, it is our safe default, and we miss a lot of chances to give real help.

Because silence is so important to us, the words which we allow to break it become even more significant. Do we rely too much on verbal truth, rather than truth expressed in music, or in dance, movement or action?

The life of the Society

Working at Friends House was at times infuriating, but generally a fascinating experience of a lively and animated body struggling to match up its experience and values as a Spirit-filled and faithful group with the need to be a properly functioning, professional organisation in British society in this century. On one occasion, Meeting for Sufferings was having difficulty with its task of setting out its aims for the next year. A Friend asked, "Can't we just go back to bumbling on in the Light?" Everyone laughed sympathetically, but we knew that the Light was actually leading us to more clarity.

We have spent years, decades, trying to perfect our organisation and our methods, and we naturally cherish the community and the institution we have built. This is the failing of every single religious institution, however loving and holy the people who try to keep it going. The corporate body becomes a purpose in itself.

Francis Howgill warned us: "If you build upon anything or have confidence in anything which stands in time and is on this side eternity and the Being of Beings, your foundation will be swept away" (QF&P 26.71). If our yearly meeting is built on anything except God, and if we find our security in anything except our shared inner meeting with God, we will be swept away.

Can we see all our committees, structures, organisations, accounts, trustee bodies, meeting houses and yearly meetings as provisional, secondary, important but not that important? Cisterns, pipelines, but not themselves the springing and flowing Spirit? The love of God is pouring out to us day by day like a huge waterfall, and we stand under it with little buckets and label them and offer them to each other. To function as a group we have to build and keep the pipelines, the organisation, but we must also respect and cherish the inner springs of life, and release them in each other rather than stop the flow.

An editor of *The Friend* once asked me what I do with my back copies; when I replied that I recycled them, she said, "Thank goodness! So many people keep every copy religiously and then write and offer them to me when they move house." Cherishing every scrap of Quaker printed material is not surprising in a group which sits round each Sunday with books in the centre of our worship space. But everything we do needs to be re-examined in the Light – does our faithful discipleship to the living Spirit require us to keep a beloved tradition, or to put it to better use in the compost heap? Or are we in fact faithful disciples of the printed word, or of the bricks of the meeting house, or of the central committee structure?

There is a dilemma here for every group of Quaker trustees, at local or national level. Their job as trustees is to safeguard the institution, to minimise risk to the corporate body, to make sure it complies with the law. This is likely to bring the trustees into conflict with those who are open to the Spirit, who want the group to take risks, who draw on our history of passionate engagement with politics and social wrongs. Here again we can learn to accept each other as different parts of the body with different functions; the clue is to acknowledge the tension and live with the difference between the varied leadings.

It is cheering that when Meeting for Sufferings, with its committee and the staff, began the task required by law of assessing the risks to the Quaker organisation, we included a careful assessment of the risks to us of not following the leadings of the Spirit. This acknowledged the tension in the task of running an organisation whose explicit task is to find the will of God and do it, but whose implicit task is frequently "Keep this body going exactly as it is".

Why do we feel it is so risky for us to grow?

Focusing on God is actually what many enquirers are looking for. A new member, who came through Quaker Quest, wrote: "There are many things about Friends that appealed to me . . . But the main thing is the effort to put God first: the acknowledgement of "that of God in everyone" and the approach to God; the focus on listening for God and discerning God's will, and the honesty, authenticity, discipline, trust and yielding involved in silently waiting on God" (*Quaker Quest News*, Autumn 2005).

❂   ❂   ❇

Maurice Creasey, the Director of Studies at Woodbrooke from 1953 to 1977, was invited to give the Swarthmore Lecture in 1969, and poured into the book and lecture the fruit of 40 years' study, reflection, prayer and worship. He told a group of Friends that he was invited by a local meeting to lead an evening's study of his book. The Clerk opened the proceedings by saying, "Well, Maurice, none of us have had time to read your book, so if you'll just sum it up for us in five minutes, we'll discuss it."

Can we take seriously and realistically the time necessary for study and reflection? As a Society without a local paid teaching ministry, we rely on ourselves and each other to read and think and speak about "the things which are eternal". Let us at least have an ideal to set before each other. John Wesley established libraries for his travelling preachers in Bristol and in London; the study of a Methodist minister today should have 30 yards of bookshelves. Even today's Anglican clergy, who rush from committee to committee, are encouraged to study in the few gaps they have. One bishop remarked, many years ago, "I can always tell when my clergy have stopped reading. If a man is a Catholic, he becomes a ritualist; if he is an Evangelical, he becomes a bigot." What does a Quaker become, when the mind goes to grass? Thank God for Woodbrooke.

Maybe a remedy here for us as a group is not so much the solitary study and reading of the separated ministry, but our shared times of discussion and growth together in our local meetings? Again, different types of Quakers need different types of learning – but doing it together can be more fun. And it's a way of exposing ourselves to the unfamiliar. We all need to keep learning.

✳   ✳   ✳

The General Synod of the Church of England met in 1992 to discuss yet again whether women could become priests. The Synod had previously agreed that such a big decision required a two-thirds majority, which was reached with a margin of two votes. When the vote was counted and the calling of the Spirit to so many women was finally accepted as worth testing, the crowds waiting outside burst out with applause and singing – and at Woodbrooke, there was a spontaneous party. Quakers everywhere welcomed the decision as a great move forward for another church and for women everywhere. We were convinced that it was right. But Quakers would not have made such a major decision with such a big minority against it.

Do Friends prize unity over truth? Do we confuse unity with unanimity, and so lose out on truth? And because we care so much for the unity of our body, do we push down in ourselves and in others the voices which speak up for the new, those who see the possibility of change and of development? Is the Quaker commandment that "thou shalt not rock the boat"?

Rowan Williams, who has his own problems in his job with holding truth and unity together, said, "I've been given a responsibility to try and care for the Church as a whole . . . People are able to learn from each other. And it's got a lot to do with valuing and nurturing unity, not as an alternative to truth, but as one of the ways we absorb truth" (*Guardian* interview, 21 March 2006).

As we talk over what Friends contribute to the wider Church, we sometimes say that we hold two treasures on behalf of the other churches, our practice of silence and our business method. This often comes across to others as "We own silence; we know all about its use in worship and our way is The Best", and "We value our business method so much that we want to impose it on you".

When the woman with the alabaster pot of ointment wanted to give something very precious to Jesus, she broke open her pot and poured out the ointment (Mark 14:3–9). So the pot didn't exist any more – it was broken – but the treasure within it had been used as it was intended, as an outpouring of love. If love asks it, we may need to break open the outward form of our treasures, to let them flow out to others.

When the charismatic movement burst on the churches in the late 1960s, we could have given so much to it, from our experience and understanding of living with the Spirit. Some individual Friends made a contribution to it, but as a body, we stood apart and missed the opportunity.

Our own inner lives

After the committee meeting, I sat with another member, a lifelong Quaker, in the corner of a country pub; I respected and valued her deeply but was rather puzzled about why she, such an artistic wordsmith, was on this committee, which was of the "roofs and drains" variety, and where I could not identify her contribution. This evening off seemed a good time to ask her. "Well, I was brought up to think that if I am asked to do something, I should trust the discernment of those asking me. I was asked to serve on this committee. I couldn't really see how I could help, but I thought I had better agree." Loving and humble, she had not trusted her own discernment that this was not a committee she could usefully serve. I felt an underlying sense that "the Society knows better than I". Maybe her self-doubt, her knowledge that as an artist she was a dubious Quaker, led her to see the invitation to serve as a stamp of approval?

I was saddened that she trusted others' discernment rather than her own; underlying this, she did not see her own worth and the worth of the gifts she could have offered to a different area of work. Can we be too humble, too trusting, too reluctant to voice our questions?

✳   ✳   ✳

"We are worried about a member of our meeting who ministers very unhelpfully."

"Have the Elders discussed it?"

"She is an Elder."

End of discussion.

"Please will those responsible for children in the Society make sure that nothing to do with war is ever mentioned to the children of our meetings?" A request to Quaker Home Service.

"We can't lay that piece of work down – it's his ministry, he'd be so upset."

Quaker worship opens us up, in a group setting, as nothing else can. Early Friends called this "tendering" – we become more tender to others, and also we ourselves become tender, hurtable, open to influences and to the Spirit, open to our own past inner hurts. So a loving Quaker meeting – or a place of work – can be a community where everyone's mental and spiritual wounds are healed because people are valued and treated with respect and straightforward truth. But the healing is not the whole aim of the worship, the meeting or the workplace; it is a side-effect, a by-product of the ordinary life of a sound community. In the same way Jesus' miracles were declarations of the coming of the Kingdom, they were not the Kingdom's main aim. A meeting is not primarily a therapeutic community. It is daily bread, not medicine.

We all value the healing, the tendering. But it's only healing when we are so healed that we can leave our illness, our wound, behind. This is difficult if our wound has guaranteed us preferential tender treatment, extra consideration, a certain self-image in the group.

Some meetings become open to manipulation by one Friend who cannot be pulled up because they would be so hurt if they were checked, so the meeting, like a family, develops strategies and ways around this which avoid addressing the issue. If the Friend consciously or half-consciously uses their vulnerability to dominate aspects of the meeting's life, they begin to blackmail the community into compliance. A book by American Friends, originally called *The Wounded Meeting*, describes various situations where this has happened, some of them outrageous, and gives some remedies (the book is now called *Dealing with Difficult Behavior in Meeting for Worship*).

In Britain Yearly Meeting we have learned over the last few years to become much more aware of this tendency, and tougher in our approach to each other. The remedies for over-tenderness are good community-building, good oversight and a shared sense of humour, so that the healing Friend can see things in proportion, can contribute their own positive good gifts, and can grow towards abundant life rather than stay in negativity.

*   *   *

How can we heal these pathological states? Hilda Clark, a doctor, wrote:

> I understand now that one's intellect alone won't pull one through, and that the greatest service it can perform is to open a window for that thing we call the divine spirit. If one trusts to it alone it's like trusting to an artificial system of ventilation – correct in theory but musty in practice. How I wish it were as easy to throw everything open to the Spirit of God as it is to fresh air.
>
> *QF&P 26.07*

Our Society is an ordinary average community, and we function well if we stick to the basic principles of good group hygiene, as an open and respectful group. But it's not just an ordinary group process. Hilda Clark learned from an understanding born of pain, which takes us back to the experience of the cross. There is a huge difference between this sort of openness to the Spirit, and thinking things through with the intellect alone.

Janey O'Shea's words to Australia Yearly Meeting in 1993 are still true:

> Renewal of the Society waits for the choice of each Friend: Am I willing to risk the disturbing, transfiguring presence of the Spirit in my life? To obey it? To expect "the Cross" and dark days as I discover and nurture who I am before God? When we choose to live the spiritual life the Quaker Way, these are the experiences we are committing ourselves to, whatever words we put upon them . . . If our collective spiritual power gathers strength, it will infect other Friends

and newcomers. Ministry will become more grounded in the Spirit and individuals will be inspired by the Spirit to serve our meetings as nurturers, prophets and conservers.

O'Shea, 2003

Is this what we want? Let us be careful what we pray for; we may get it.

11. What helps Me?

The end of words is to bring us to the knowledge of things which words cannot utter.

Isaac Penington, *QF&P* 27.27

Everyday practice

So what do I do? What helps me?

Each stage of life presents its own challenges – and its own opportunities for developing our understanding of God. What about the terribly busy stage when small children take up almost every waking minute ? We had four children with two years between each, so the first few years were full. It was essential at this stage, I found, to see God in the busyness, in the caring and activity, rather than fight to find a place for God outside it. Go with and use the rhythms of your life as it is. Work with what you've got, not with what you wish you had. Learn and reflect on the lessons your own experience teaches you about God's total involvement in the world. So many people write of God's care simply as they receive it. Parents of small children understand God's self-giving care, poured out endlessly and unquestioningly.

As the children grow, so we also understand God's longing for us to grow, to develop and become our own independent selves, because that is what we want for our children. As I learnt about management of a work group, I understood how different this is from the family group; the aim of the office team is to be there and to focus our efforts together on a shared task; the aim of the family group is for each person to find their own separate life focus and leave – and God wants this for us too. The teenage Ronald Knox, son of the evangelical Bishop of Manchester, is said to have written in his diary, "I must have a religion, and it must be different from Father's." Did George Fox feel the same about his father, "righteous Christer", the churchwarden? Our children, part of the boomerang generation, first go, then come back and then leave again, physically and spiritually.

So I learnt to aim at independence for each child, and to use the everyday household jobs as times of prayer – washing up, scrubbing the floor. Hanging out the washing early in the morning was a good time to "lift up my eyes to the hills" – especially when we lived near Dartmoor. Cooking for the family and for guests is a good time to think ahead to the sacramental meal we will share and the situation of each person round the table. Husband and wife's shared cherishing in lovemaking bears a warmly flowering fruit in the home's loving, happy and welcoming atmosphere. The first letter of John simply states the experience of many couples, gay and straight: "God is love, and those who live in love live in God, and God lives in them" (1 John 4:16). I was kept going by friendships, by the mutual support of other mothers in the same situation, by occasional times when I was taken away from the nappies, by grandparents taking the children occasionally.

How do I share my practice? I don't. Peter and I practise alongside each other rather than together. We tried to have a quiet time together but it didn't work. There is a lovely description of a Quaker couple, Gwen and Corder Catchpool, in the early years of their married life: "twice a day, hand in hand, they sought in prayerful silence for God's guidance" (Hughes, 1964). Some Friends can do this – but we are a different couple. But the fact that we each have a daily routine of reading and prayer helps us both, and occasionally we talk about this as we do about other aspects of our shared life. We are careful to keep total confidentiality about people who talk privately with either of us; so I know as little as possible about those who come to Peter for spiritual direction, and he had plenty to think about without knowing the details of Friends House business.

We start each day with a pot of tea in bed, Bible reading and prayer for people we know. I also read through *Quaker Faith & Practice*; I just keep five markers in the book, roughly evenly spaced, and each day I read the next passage at each marker. When I was working at Friends House, I needed to know it well, and this is a good way to get to grips with it systematically. It is so full of richness – you meet so many people! But when I was a teenager, and had just been given my copy of the old blue book, *Christian Faith & Practice*, I just used to open it at random and read what I wanted. When we're on holiday, or on a day we wake up late or have to get up very early, the routine can be cut short – it's adaptable, like a fitness regime.

I am systematic in praying for people because that's how I work – that's my type. Steadily and regularly turning the flow of light and energy in the direction of a person, a project or a situation is good. I find a list of people to pray for is useful, and also a list of international situations; this makes sure I don't miss people out. I also use the *Book of Meetings* as a prayer list; I started doing so as part of my work. I don't feel great emotions doing this, any more than I feel huge emotions when I'm doing routine housework – perhaps I just lead a very grey life all round. But this method seems to develop a sustained awareness of people.

It's also good to hold wordlessly in the Light the situations and people we all come across every day. The ambulance or police car going past, with the people it is going to and its driver; the international meeting in the news; the howling child and angry mother in the supermarket; the distraught person on the news bulletin and all the invisible others they represent.

What do we do when we pray for people? We push energy in their direction; and when we pray together, we combine that energy. I remember a time when our Land Rover was stuck in a muddy field. Dad got us all at the back of it, he shouted "push", we all pushed together and with a heave it was out. That's the feeling of concerted prayer about a situation that is stuck – we link our energies together. Can Friends accept leadership and direction of this sort, as we hold a situation in the Light? Do we agree on the direction we are pushing in?

Perhaps another metaphor for our shared prayer expresses our experience better. We hold between us a situation which is like a tangled ball of string; pulling it or pushing it won't actually loosen the knots. We can hold it gently, loosening it together so that the twists release their tension, letting go of knotted feelings, letting in air and flexibility so that we can all see how to sort it out. Here we are examining where the energy is going in unhelpful directions, and releasing it to be more productive.

Another image might be plunging people into the abyss of God.

And what am I holding in the Light when I think of someone? I sometimes picture "that of God" in them like a squiggle of light inside them, their inner essence, their essential being, which I focus on and hold in God's light for a blessing. It's particularly useful to do this when we "uphold the Clerk" in a Quaker business meeting while they are writing a difficult minute, or in the quiet before the business starts. The Clerk is totally engaged, in the depths of their being; all their essential and particular talents and gifts are at the service of the meeting; they have no spare energy for attention to the Spirit, so at that point they need to draw on our energy to hold them at depth.

Meeting for worship, one of our most significant experiences, is a time when we all feel connected and related to each other and to God, so I find that when I think of people in their relationships, I hold in the Light the threads of connection between them, like strands of wool. I find I do this especially with the howling child in the supermarket. The medium the Spirit will use at this point is the relationship between the child and the parent, so this is what needs to be creative and positive. The Holy Spirit, in Christian experience, is a sense of community, of fellowship, of links in the connecting web of friendship and love. "The web is the love that flows through creation, from G-d/ess, from us, from everywhere. The web is an affirmation and comfort, support and clear-naming . . . Most of all, for me, the web is friendship" (*QF&P* 26.35). All the symbols of the Spirit – air, fire, water, doves – are moving, fluid, they can't be confined or pinned down. Prayer similarly can flow and move in a flash as quick as radio waves or computer messages.

I've also learned to use the energy of my own mind more productively. For years, a certain person in the public eye used to irritate me beyond measure, so that whenever his name came up in the paper or on TV I would get cross with him. Then I realised I was wasting a lot of negative energy like this, and decided to turn it into positive energy, so when I heard his name I mentally blessed him. I'm not sure what it did for him but it was much better for me. We can choose how to use our mental energy, positively or negatively.

The discipline here is not just having a regular time, but reflecting on it occasionally and making sure that what we do accords with our concept of God. Living with someone who has a similar understanding is a great help. If we are alone in our understanding of the Divine, can we talk in our meetings or with a friend about these matters? Some Friends have rediscovered the value of spiritual friendship.

Learning the How of prayer as well as the What and Why is part of learning its technology, and as we see how people's inner lives have developed over the centuries, we can see how each new technology has been taken up into our discipline. In the middle ages, new techniques of building, fresco painting and glazing led to shared devotion and discipline, as people made and looked at the mediaeval wall paintings and stained glass in churches. Later, printing made the Bible easily available, so people developed a discipline of individual reading, rather than the communal reading of the monastic orders, and the "Daily Chapter" or daily portion with commentary became common. Today, can we explore how to use film or music in meditation and prayer together? There are all sorts of possibilities.

What use are we making of today's technology? Some people use the time when their computer is booting up for a moment of centring down. As we pray for individuals, it can be easier to use a handheld computer or a laptop, rather than paper lists. People's needs change, so the listing changes. Your son and his partner are getting married – you pray for the wedding. Then they tell you they are having a baby – so you add Tadpole to the list. They find out it's a boy – Tadpole changes to boy Tadpole – they choose a name, so you are praying for your grandchild by name – an exciting move! As the time gets closer you add prayers for the birth, and so on.

But this is solitary – what of the potential of information technology for linking us in worship and prayer? There is a meeting for worship on the web, at http://worship.quaker.org, which is made up of about 100 people all over the world. This is a "Meeting" in every sense. The Church of England recently set up its first cyber-parish, which now has 500 members, shared prayer and discussion, and 75–100 messages a day. The Irish Jesuits have perhaps the most developed Internet prayer space at www.sacredspace.ie. There are tremendous possibilities here.

Whether we use books, buildings or computers, what we could call the technology of the body is one of the most basic things to learn – how to use breath, mind, posture to develop and deepen our inner lives. Quaker experience of practising physical stillness could teach others – can we make our knowledge explicit for ourselves first?

Accepting the simplicity

My own experience has been of growing up in a Quaker family and a meeting, learning at university many of the fundamental truths of the Christian faith without having to unlearn childish concepts of too many of them, and then filling them out with experience in a life necessarily based on them because of our family's professional work in the Society of Friends and the Church of England. As I've developed my own travelling document, some things which I thought essential have been discarded; others have become more important. I believe more and more in less and less; I've travelled towards simplicity.

At the centre is a fundamental, tested belief in God, and in the primacy of God's action. By "God" I mean the energy flowing through all the created universe, beyond us all and yet at the same time giving God's nature to be known – transcendent yet immanent, loving yet full of truth, eternal, outside time yet working in time, the source of all that is, yet incarnate, given particular voice and form in Jesus yet also a light within every person, a powerful transforming Spirit, fluid, elusive, which is also a still small voice asking for our co-operation in cherishing real overflowing abundant life in every single thing.

Because of this, we can be held securely and confidently in our deepest being. The essence of each of us is held in God. The Quaker words which best sum up my confidence come from George Hodgkin, a Friend from the centre of the walled garden of families and meetings, who died on a relief mission in Baghdad in 1918:

> So much of life is just going on and going on, long after the excitement and stimulus has faded . . . We must give up trying to hold God's hand, and just stretch out our hands – even if they are just fists – for God to hold. There is all the difference between holding and being held . . . The thing is just to live the highest life we know and leave everything else.
>
> *CF&P* 106, 105

If God is God, we can be totally confident, but we must rely only on God, not on anything else. We cannot rely on individual Friends, or on Quaker thinking, on our beloved Quaker structures or institutions, on our buildings or on our famous business method. This is where Quaker principles themselves direct us away from Quakerism; we hold within ourselves and in our tradition the truthful ruthless critique of that tradition, and we must hear it, we must be open to new Light, and to new reflections of the old.

Holding on to anything temporal leads us to idolatry, to putting something made by human beings in the place of God. William Temple said "The Church that lives for itself will be sure to die by itself" (quoted in Green, 2001). We need to look for the loving energy, the abundant life which flows through the things we have made, the structures we have built, the committees we have worked so hard for, the meeting houses we have cherished, the communities we have built up. They do not exist for themselves, and if we create them for themselves they will become monuments and tombstones weighing down our own new rising life.

I saw this most clearly when at the time of my father's death I realised that much of my confidence was based in him, not in the greater Life beyond himself on which he was focused. I also used to see it when my mother sat in Meeting and turned away from focusing on us, her children, to attend to the inner spring of the Spirit within her. We can learn so much from each other's faces in Meeting. Dante sees it when at the end of his poem his beloved Beatrice leads him to the vision of God, and finally turns away from him to God. "And then she turned to the eternal fountain" (Canto 31.93). In the end all those who lead us to God leave us alone. The words we rely on go into silence; our solid foundation is the flowing fountain of life.

After Teresa of Avila's death, a slip of paper was found in her prayer book, in her handwriting:

> Nada te turbe
> nada te espante
> todo se pasa
> Dios no se muda
> La paciencia
> todo lo alcanza
> Quién a Dios tiene
> nada le falta
> sólo Dios basta
>
> Nothing disturb you,
> nothing affright you;
> all things are passing,
> God never changes.
> Patient endurance
> can achieve everything.
> Whoever has God
> can want for nothing;
> alone God suffices.

12. Living in the Life of the Spirit

> These are only hints and guesses,
> Hints followed by guesses; and the rest
> Is prayer, observance, discipline, thought and action.
> The hint half guessed, the gift half understood, is Incarnation.

T.S. Eliot, "The Dry Salvages"

A few years ago, at Mount Grace Priory in Yorkshire, several tons of earth were moved during restoration work. Old soil which had not been exposed to the air for centuries was uncovered and the seeds of mediaeval plants, hidden in it 400 years ago, began to grow. Wale, a yellow dye herb, sprang up. We read about this and visited the Priory. I expected to see some rather tired and sad-looking plants, which had germinated half-heartedly and crawled out of the earth. Instead, we found masses of tall vibrant flower-spikes, blooming, glowing golden, bursting with life – perfectly ready to take their part again in the cycle of creation. The power of the seed was not diminished in any way by being hidden for so long in the dark ground.

The poppies bloomed in Flanders fields, in the First World War, for just the same reason: when all the trenches were dug and shellfire ploughed up the fallow ground, the earth was exposed to the light and poppy seeds were given just the right conditions for their growth. How many of the soldiers were cheered by their beauty? Were some of them angry that such an affirmation of life could spring up there alongside the squalor and terror? The gift of new life even from destruction and darkness is part of the pattern of our world, part of the ground of our being.

Living faithfully in a shifting world, as we ourselves are growing and transforming, can be confusing; we feel that the ground moves under our feet, especially if the patterns, structure and thinking of our religious body are changing. "Isn't this group supposed to hold me firmly?" we say in our hearts. Francis Howgill spoke strongly in 1656:

> If you build upon anything or have confidence in anything
> which stands in time and is on this side eternity and the Being

of Beings, your foundation will be swept away . . . Why gad you abroad? Why trim you yourselves with the saints' words, when you are ignorant of the Life? Return, return to Him that is the first Love, and the first-born of every creature, who is the Light of the world . . . Return home to within, and here you will see your Teacher not removed into a corner, but present when you are upon your beds and about your labour, convincing, instructing, leading, correcting, judging and giving peace to all that love and follow Him.

QF&P 26.71

The foundation of our silence, the ground of our action and thinking and organisation, is God, at home within us. Francis Howgill gives his own answers to our questions about how we create our inner life. His overriding concern is not his own development, but what God is doing in him. If we can see the gift half understood as God implicit, indwelling and immanent in all of our nature, then "what God is doing in me" and "finding the best in my nature and living by it" are two ways of describing the same thing. And the Divine is not only immanent; God is also transcendent, bigger than our thinking and our natures; different, though not distant.

Jesus described the relationship we can all have with the Spirit of God, the Spirit of truth: "The wind blows where it chooses, and you hear the sound of it, but you do not know where it comes from or where it goes. So it is with everyone who is born of the Spirit" (John 3:8). We catch the hint half guessed as the Spirit sparkles within our hearts and we create afresh, as we see the vision of a peaceful world, as we realise our own power to give and to grow.

> Ah! the bird of heaven!
> Follow where the bird has gone;
> Ah! the bird of heaven!
> Keep on travelling on.

We keep on travelling on, alongside the other people who are given us by the Spirit, awkward as some of them may be to us – and probably they find us just as difficult. James Nayler was convinced that the Spirit's "ground and spring is the mercies and forgiveness of

God" (*QF&P* 19.12). God's mercy is the fluid foundation of the Spirit's committed, solid, promised and reliable love, overflowing and pouring out for all of us. In the variety of our individual natures and of the world, we make this real for each other in mutual forgiveness, in loving, truthful, accepting and challenging communities. This Spirit is the ground of our meetings and of our confidence.

Our image of the Spirit as a spring includes a strong element of tension – the tension of feeling called, of being asked to move, to stand up, to be seen and heard as voices of the future, as signs of life, as merciful, forgiving people. When we are forgiven, when we forgive others, things change and move – and this can be difficult to live with; it's so much easier if we can give people a permanent label because they have done something, or not done something. But if they respond to their own discoveries about themselves, the light of God within them, if they grow and change, can we respond too? If we are all changed and forgiven together in our shared travelling, do we feel unsettled, or can we be glad?

We feel "the mercies and forgiveness of God" as the resilient spring of the Spirit within us. Some of us feel the strong tensed coil of goodwill, bursting with quiet and restrained energy, ready to jump to action, longing to show the world the fruit of real peace. Some of us feel the lively inner seed, ready to spring into new life, new creation. Some of us sense the bubbling and welling up of Love in our quiet hours of silence, an inner flooding of the wellsprings of our hearts with energy which we turn to discernment, to prayer, to deep understanding, to thinking and reflection. It's hard to tell what is us and what is the work of God within us – but we know we are invited to co-operate: not to quench the Spirit, but to be part of the flow of love in our time.

Seeing the Spirit as water, in another metaphor, we can feel our cool stillness, and the calming pace of our procedures, as fresh cold water; though as we follow our leadings, our peace and justice work will undoubtedly get us into hot water too.

Abandoning metaphor, my answer to "God, who are you?" is that we live our lives alongside a lively Spirit, a big Spirit whom we stretch our minds to grasp, and whom we can reach for best together, sharing our different understandings in the abundant life of which Jesus spoke. This Spirit is both active and quiet, peaceful and dynamic, ordered, settled, and creative, homely and gigantic. When I ask "God, who am I?" I conclude that we all live and move and have our being in this Spirit, and in the physical and mental universes which are the Spirit's expression of enormous, explosive and exuberant life.

As we seek to be faithful disciples of the Spirit, resting, rock-solid, on something totally fluid, totally hidden, we find that we have to live with provisional answers to many questions. Grounding our lives in God's forgiveness and mercy, we pass this on to others in the flow of community life; living in this fluidity takes skill, and we can help each other to develop and grow. We can work out our "travelling documents" for ourselves, and learn from each other's discoveries. Working with and learning alongside children and young people in our meetings helps them and simultaneously helps us to grow ourselves; talking with people who come to us asking about Quaker thinking and practice is essential, and keeps our own thoughts lively, connected and fresh. What is the new language that we will use in the next few decades of this century? What new music will we compose, what new words are springing from our hearts?

Our current practice and our tradition both contain their own correctives against fossilisation and stagnation. Friend after Friend from our past directs us to the lively Spirit working afresh within us. Week by week the amazing fact of Quaker worship teaches us quietly how to enter the world in our heart, how to wait upon God, how to listen to the inward teacher, and how to watch for the hints and guesses, the sparkles along the web of our community.

In our silence, what is God doing?
How can we help?

Questions for Thought and Discussion

Some of these are suitable for reflective discussion, of a worship-sharing type; others are for individual reflection; some are for practical consideration, perhaps finishing with a meeting decision.

John Woolman suggested that we should live "answerable to the design of our creation".

- What is the design of the individual inner creation of each of us, what sort of person am I? How can I find this out?
- Can I explore this in the quiet of meeting for worship and by myself? Or will I find myself more easily in a group?
- What do I create? Children, an atmosphere, a garden, music, a good place of work, peace?
- What do I contribute – what is my gift? How does this vary from context to context, over time and situation?
- What helps my individual inner life? What hinders it?
- In order to be single-minded, integrated, pure in heart in this search, what do I need to lay aside?
- How do I live most in accord with my own nature? What re-creates me?
- Who helps me to build the strength and integrity of my inner being? What group, what people?
- Can I help others, and can others help me, in loving honesty to know and accept ourselves more fully?
- What can we do, as part of the international and national community, to renew and re-create our Earth?
- What can I do as an individual? What can my meeting do?

* * *

A new member wrote:

> There are many things about Friends that appealed to
> me . . . But the main thing is the effort to put God first:
> the acknowledgement of "that of God in everyone", and
> the approach to God; the focus on listening for God and
> discerning God's will, and the honesty, authenticity, discipline,
> trust and yielding involved in silently waiting on God.

- How do we put God first?
- How do we keep our picture of God big enough?
- How do we enlarge our understanding of the Spirit's action in other faiths, and in people who say they have no faith?
- In the quiet of Meeting, can we explore what we build upon and have confidence in? Can we look beyond that thing or person to the divine strength at the heart?
- Can we give people and things back to God, their source and origin?
- Is there anything in our Quaker structure or life which we are making into an idol, something in the place of the Divine?
- Are we building new Quaker structures on this solid foundation of faith in the living Spirit?
- Are we willing to be built with? – to be the materials and tools of creation?
- Who is putting into words the thinking and framework we need to keep ourselves and our structures grounded in the Spirit at local and national level? Does this seem important to me? Why, or why not?
- When we disagree with one another, do we struggle to hear where the other's words are coming from, and to search for constructive ways forward together?
- We know our values – do we truly live by them in our meetings?

✳   ✳   ✳

George Fox asked Margaret Fell and the people of Ulverston: "What canst thou say? Art thou a child of Light, and hast walked in the Light . . . ?" (*QF&P* 19.07)

- What is your language, your way of communicating truth?
- What is your experience of the Spirit?
- How do you reply to the newcomer who asks, "So what do you believe?"
- What central truths and values do we need to pass on to young people and children in our meetings?
- What are the new things we will be saying in the next half century – what music will Friends compose, what language is springing from our hearts?

✸　✸　✸

James Nayler wrote in 1660, "There is a spirit which I feel . . . its ground and spring is the mercies and forgiveness of God . . . " (*QF&P* 19.12).

- How do the mercy and forgiveness of God spring up in our lives?
- How do we ground our lives in this fluidity?
- Can we accept God's confidence in us?
- Can we encourage each other to know that confidence?

Glossary

Quaker organisation

Britain Yearly Meeting is the body of Friends in Britain, made up of **monthly meetings** (area units) and **preparative** (local) **meetings**. "Yearly Meeting" and "Monthly Meeting" also denote the annual and monthly meetings of Friends for worship and business.

Meeting for Sufferings is the central deliberative body of Britain YM, acting on behalf of the yearly meeting between its annual sessions.

Quaker Faith & Practice (*QF&P*) is the latest (1994) in a series of Books of Discipline of Quakers in Britain, dating from 1738. It combines sections on the structure of Britain YM, its meetings, committees, office-holders and ways of working, with an anthology of Friends' descriptions of their experience of, or beliefs about, all aspects of their faith and practice. It is prefaced by the 42 *Advices & Queries*, encapsulating Friends' search for life in the Spirit. Quoting from a seventeenth-century minute of Quakers in Balby, *QF&P* and *Advices & Queries* begin with the assurance that "these things we do not lay upon you as a rule or form of life to walk by, but that all, with the measure of light which is pure and holy, may be guided; . . . for the letter killeth, but the Spirit giveth life." ***Christian Faith & Practice*** is the 1959 predecessor of *QF&P*.

Testimonies embody the values of Quakerism in practices like peace work, simplicity of life and the pursuit of integrity. The **Peace Testimony** is famously expressed in a declaration to Charles II of 1660, found in *QF&P* 24.04.

Quaker meetings

Meeting for worship takes place at least weekly in most local meetings, being open to any, members and non-members, who wish to attend. **Meetings for business** are equally rooted in worship, but are focused on specific matters for consideration and decision.

Elders are appointed by local, monthly, yearly and other Quaker meetings to take particular responsibility for the spiritual wellbeing of the meeting and its members. **Overseers** are similarly appointed for pastoral oversight. The meeting **Clerk** has the responsibility for the agenda of a business meeting elsewhere laid on a chairperson; since Quakers do not vote but rather wait for a united "sense of the meeting" to emerge, however, the Clerk has a very particular role in discerning and minuting the emergence of this shared decision.

Attenders are those who frequently attend Meeting, though they have not come into membership. Attenders are often deeply-rooted and take a significant part in Quaker life.

Some Quaker organisations

Appleseed was initiated by Chris Cook and Brenda Clifft Heales as a ministry offering weekends, retreats and other events, mainly at Woodbrooke, combining head learning and heart learning with simple arts-based response activities and worship-sharing rather than discussion.

The Leaveners are the Quaker Youth Theatre, their name coming from biblical imagery beloved of early Friends.

Quaker Quest provides an experiential introduction to Quaker thinking and practice for newcomers, with a cycle of sessions on basic aspects.

The Quaker Tapestry is a series of panels depicting Quaker life, past and present, embroidered by groups and individuals, working cooperatively across the yearly meeting. It is permanently on display in Kendal Meeting House, Cumbria.

Woodbrooke, the Quaker Study Centre in Birmingham, teaches and publishes in all areas of Quaker faith and practice.

Some projects with Quaker involvement

The Alternatives to Violence Project (AVP) organises workshops which empower people to lead nonviolent lives, based on respecting and caring for ourselves and others. Though Quaker in its origins and ethos, it is composed of people of all faiths or none.

Circles of Support & Accountability originated in Canada in the 1990s, then were brought to the UK by Quakers. Operating on the principle of a restorative, non-punitive justice, they work with volunteers to support and supervise people with convictions for sex offences in their safe reintegration to the community.

Conscience: The Peace Tax Campaign campaigns for the legal right for those with a conscientious objection to war to have the military part of their taxes spent on peacebuilding initiatives.

The Ecumenical Accompaniment Programme in Palestine and Israel (EAPPI) recruits volunteers to accompany Palestinians and Israelis in their nonviolent actions and concerted advocacy efforts to end the occupation.

Bibliography

Advices & Queries. London: Britain Yearly Meeting, 1995. See also
    Quaker Faith & Practice, of which it forms the first chapter.

Ambler, Rex, *Truth of the Heart: an anthology of George Fox 1624–1691*.
    London: Quaker Books, 2001.

Ambler, Rex, *Light to Live By: an exploration in Quaker spirituality*.
    London: Quaker Books, 2002.

Bauman, Richard, *Let Your Words be Few: the symbolism of speaking
    and silence among seventeenth-century Quakers*. London: QHS,
    1998 (first published Cambridge University Press, 1983).

Bible:
    New Revised Standard Version (NRSV). Oxford University Press,
        1989.
    Gaus, Andy (trans), *The Unvarnished New Testament*. Grand
        Rapids, MI: Phanes Press, 1991.

Blackadder, Jill Slee: see *Quakerism, a way of life*.

Bonhoeffer, Dietrich, *Letters and Papers from Prison*, ed Eberhard
    Bethge. First published in English 1953. London: SCM, 1956; New
    York: Touchstone, 1997.

Book of Common Prayer, first published 1662 by Oxford University
    Press.

Boulton, David (ed), *Godless for God's Sake: nontheism in contemporary
    Quakerism*. Dent: Dale Historical Monographs, 2006.

Carter, Sydney, *Green Print for Song*. London: Stainer & Bell Ltd, 1974.

*Christian Faith & Practice: the book of Christian discipline of the Yearly
    Meeting of the Religious Society of Friends (Quakers) in Britain
    (CF&P)*. London: Britain Yearly Meeting, 1959. See also *Quaker
    Faith & Practice*.

Dante, Alighieri, trans C.H. Sisson, *The Divine Comedy*. Oxford
    University Press, 1993 (The World's Classics).

Dealing with Difficult Behavior in Meeting for Worship. Philadelphia:
    Friends General Conference Ministry and Nurture Committee, rev
    ed 2002; previous ed 1993 titled *The Wounded Meeting*.

The Dream of the Rood: see Kennedy, C.

The English Hymnal. First published 1906; 2nd edition, Oxford University Press, 1933.

Equipping for Ministry: a national conference for Friends. Birmingham and London: Woodbrooke and Quaker Home Service, 1990.

Fox, George, *A Collection of Epistles*, 1698. In *Works of George Fox* (8 vols). PA: New Foundation/George Fox Fund, 1990.

Fox, George, *Journal* (1652), ed J.L. Nickalls. Cambridge University Press, 1952. Reprinted Philadelphia: Religious Society of Friends, 1985.

Fox, George: *see also* Ambler, Rex

Glazer, Daphne, *Trespass and Trust: Quaker Meetings and sex offenders.* London: Quaker Books, 2004.

Green, Michael, *Adventure of Faith: Reflections on 50 years of Christian Service.* Grand Rapids, MI: Zondervan Publishing Company, 2001.

Heales, Brenda Clifft, and Chris Cook, *Images and Silence: the future of Quaker ministry.* London: Quaker Home Service, 1992 (Swarthmore Lecture).

Hopkins, Gerard Manley, *The Major Works*, ed Catherine Phillips. Oxford University Press, 2002 (The World's Classics).

Hughes, William R., *Indomitable Friend: Corder Catchpool 1883–1952.* London: Housmans, 1964.

Kennedy, Charles, *Early English Poetry: translated into alliterative verse.* New York: Oxford University Press, 1963.

Kierkegaard, Søren, *Purity of Heart is to will one thing: spiritual preparation for the office of confession,* trans Douglas Steere. Glasgow: Fontana Books, 1961.

Lawrence, Brother of the Resurrection, *The Practice of the Presence of God.* Llandeilo: Cygnus Books, 1999.

Lewis, C.S., *The Lion, the Witch and the Wardrobe* (1950). William Collins Sons & Co. Ltd, 1987.

Lewis, C.S., *Collected Letters, volume 1, Family Letters 1905–1931,* ed Walter Hooper. London: HarperCollins, 2000.

Loring, Patricia, *Listening Spirituality*: vol 1, *Personal Spiritual Practices*; vol 2, *Corporate Spiritual Practice among Friends.* Washington DC: Openings Press, 1997 and 1999.

MacGregor, Neil, *Seeing Salvation: images of Christ in art.* BBC Worldwide, 2000.

Moorman, J.R.H., *St Francis of Assisi.* London: SPCK, 1963.

Muers, Rachel, *Keeping God's Silence: towards a theological ethics of communication*. Oxford: Blackwell, 2004.

O'Shea, Janey, *Living the Way*. London: Quaker Books, 2003.

Penington, Isaac, *Knowing the Mystery of Life Within: selected writings of Isaac Penington*, edited by Rosemary Moore and Mel Keizer. London: Quaker Books, 2005.

Penn, William, *Fruits of a father's love*, 1726, pp 47–48; reprinted as "The advice of William Penn to his children" in William Penn, *A Collection of the Works* , 1726, vol 1, p 899; *Select Works*, 1782, vol 5, p 448. *Fruits of a father's love* is reprinted in *William Penn on Religion and Ethics*, 2 vols ed Hugh S. Barbour. Lewiston NY: Edwin Mellen Press, 1991; vol 2, pp.629–648.

Piety Promoted, in a collection of the dying sayings of many of the people called Quakers [by John Tomkins]. London: Tace Sowle, 1706. Priscilla Cotton entry p. 60.

Postgate, Oliver, *Seeing Things: an autobiography*. Pan, 2001; "Agapé" originally published as a poem card by Menard Press, 1985, printed here as subsequently amended by the author.

Quaker Faith & Practice: the book of Christian discipline of the Yearly Meeting of the Religious Society of Friends (Quakers) in Britain (QF&P). Britain Yearly Meeting, 1995. See also *Christian Faith & Practice*

Quakerism, a way of life: in homage to Sigrid Helliesen Lund on her 90th birthday, ed Hans Eirik Aarek. Norway: Kvekerforlaget, 1982. Contains Jill Slee Blackadder's poem "The Rainbow".

Richardson, Alan, *Creeds in the Making: a short introduction to the history of Christian doctrine*. London: SCM Press, 1935.

Robinson, John, *Honest to God*. London: SCM Press, 1963.

Robson, S.M., "An Exploration of Conflict Handling among Quakers" (unpublished thesis). University of Huddersfield, 2005.

Sawtell, Roger and Susan, *Reflections from a Long Marriage*. London: Quaker Books, 2006 (Swarthmore Lecture).

Soelle, Dorothee and Schottroff, Luise, *Jesus of Nazareth*, trans John Bowden. Louisville, KY: Westminster John Knox Press, 2002.

Taber, Bill, *Four Doors to Meeting for Worship*. Wallingford PA: Pendle Hill, 1992 (Pendle Hill Pamphlet 306).

Taber, Fran, *Come Aside and Rest Awhile*. Wallingford PA: Pendle Hill, 1997. (Pendle Hill Pamphlet 335).

This I Affirm. London: Quaker Home Service, 1999 (special issue of periodical *Reaching Out*).

Tolkien, J.R.R., *Tree & Leaf* (1964). London: HarperCollins, 2001.

Tolkien, J.R.R., *The Lord of the Rings* (1954). London: HarperCollins, 2005.

Towards a Quaker View of Sex: an essay by a group of Friends. London: Friends Home Service Committee, 1963.

Twelve Quakers and Evil. London: Quaker Quest, 2005.

Vining, Elizabeth G., *Friend of Life: the Biography of Rufus M. Jones*. Philadelphia and New York: Lippincott, 1958.

Williamson, Marianne, *A Return to Love*. London: HarperCollins, 1992.

Wink, Walter, *Naming the Powers: the language of power in the New Testament*. Philadelphia: Fortress Press, 1984.

Wink, Walter, *Engaging the Powers: discernment and resistance in a world of domination*. Minneapolis: Fortress Press, 1992.

Wink, Walter, *Unmasking the Powers: the invisible forces that determine human existence*. Philadelphia: Fortress Press, 1993.

Woolman, John, ed Moulton, Phillip P., *The Journal and Major Essays of John Woolman*. New York: Oxford University Press, 1971.

The Wounded Meeting: see *Dealing with Difficult Behavior in Meeting for Worship*

Yamamoto, Yukitaka, *Kami no Michi: the way of the Kami*. Stockton, CA: Tsubaki America Publications Department, Stockton, 1999.